Raising Money by Mail

Strategies for growth and financial stability

Mal Warwick

The New, Revised Edition of *Revolution in the Mailbox*

STRATHMOOR
PRESS

Printed in the United States of America.

ISBN 0-9624891-6-6

Published in 1994 by Strathmoor Press. For more information, write or call:
Strathmoor Press
2550 Ninth Street, Suite 1000
Berkeley CA 94710-2516
(510) 843-8888
Strathmoor Press is a subsidiary of Changing America, Inc.

10 9 8 7 6 5 4 3 2 1

Also by Mal Warwick

contents

a few words of thanks

T'S ALL RON DELLUMS' FAULT. I got into the direct mail business fifteen years ago to help Congressman Dellums launch a nationwide fundraising campaign. Because he insisted I personally supervise the consultants we'd hired, I got a taste of direct mail fundraising at its very best—and I was hooked for life.

Since those exhilarating days in the fall of 1979, when I was often up in the middle of the night, counting the checks rolling into the Dellums campaign, I've worked with hundreds of not-for-profit causes and institutions and five Presidential campaigns. My coworkers and I have raised well over $100 million to promote human dignity and democracy. In the process, I've come to know hundreds of supremely talented individuals who have committed years of their lives to make the world a better place—a list of people far too long to reproduce here. They, my clients, ultimately deserve any credit I may get for writing this book.

I am very grateful to one client in particular for directly contributing to this project. Sylvia Siegel, founder of TURN (Toward Utility Rate Normalization), and Audrie Krause, TURN's current Executive Director, graciously gave their permission for me to reproduce the direct mail fundraising packages in Chapter 6.

I'm also greatly indebted to the more than 150 friends and colleagues in Mal Warwick & Associates, The Progressive Group, and our affiliated companies who made possible the first edition of this book in 1989. They were an extraordinarily dedicated bunch, and I am privileged to have worked by their side. A few deserve special mention here.

■ Without the help of Stephen Hitchcock, now President of Mal Warwick & Associates, I could not have written *Raising Money by Mail*. The wisdom Steve has gained in more than twenty years as a professional fundraiser has found its way into nearly every chapter of this book.

■ Royce Kelley, then a Senior Consultant at Mal Warwick & Associates, helped me organize the material that became the first edition. He was also of great help on the illustrations, some of which he produced. You'll find this book much more useful because Royce put so much time into it.

■ My good friends at The Progressive Group, cofounder and President Joseph H. White, Jr., and Vice President Bernadette Ferguson, made key contributions. Without their obliging support, the insight they offered, and the illustrations they provided, it would have been impossible to cover telephone fundraising in this book.

Several others, including a series of resourceful assistants, lent a hand in this project: Eric Oliver, who served as my research assistant for the first edition; Ina Cooper, who reviewed the original text, page by page, to ferret out errors; and now Mwosi Swenson, who performed a dozen essential tasks, always with grace, good humor, and extraordinary skill.

For all the many important contributions that others have made to this book, none of them bears any responsibility for its contents. I've borrowed a great many ideas, but the words and images on these pages were all mine except where I've indicated otherwise. Now they're yours, too—and welcome to them!

introduction

FOLLOWING WORLD WAR II, the Easter Seal Society and a few other big American charities began making extensive use of the mails to meet their increasingly ambitious fundraising goals. With little cash outlay, they mailed millions of inexpensive fundraising letters and consistently reaped huge profits.

So successful were these early mass-mail fundraising efforts that some charities simply banked the proceeds without bothering to record the contributors' names and addresses. It was cheaper to send out virtually the same appeal again the next year to the same millions of addresses.

That was nearly half a century ago. A great deal has happened since: a more than twenty-fold increase in charitable contributions, the advent of ZIP codes and mainframe computers, fundraising scandals on network news, flexible personal computers, 800% inflation in nonprofit postal rates, and a comparable rise in printing costs—and, above all, *competition* in the form of appeals mailed by thousands upon thousands of nonprofit groups both large and small.

In 1993, the U.S. Postal Service distributed more than 12 *billion* pieces of mail at discounted nonprofit bulk rates—most of them appeals for funds—plus uncounted numbers of first- and second-class (newspaper) mailing rates. Direct mail fundraising accounts for a major share of the support given many of our country's biggest charities, and it looms large on the political landscape as well.

This proliferation of mail has created a challenge for nonprofit organizations to make profits through direct mail. To help meet this challenge, hundreds of consulting firms have come into existence, offering a staggering variety of approaches and levels of skill. Now, more than forty years into its history, direct mail fundraising has gotten *complicated*.

The pages ahead are my attempt to explain some of the complications.

■ ■ ■ ■

I wrote *Raising Money by Mail* in response to years of seeing desperate and bewildered looks on the faces of clients, employees, and friends. These looks are often justified. Many direct mail fundraising "experts" go out of their way to mystify the process. There are also things about this craft that are inherently confusing. In fact, some are downright illogical. I hope the following pages help demystify this crazy business and cast a little light on some of its counterintuitive aspects.

While excellent books have been written about direct mail, and even about direct mail fundraising in particular, only a few are useful to the general reader. Many of the others are technical discussions laden with statistical formulas and bearing a disturbing resemblance to treatises on mechanical engineering. There are also several books about writing good fundraising letters (including, *ahem!*, my own, *How to Write Successful Fundraising Letters*). Books on letter-writing may boost your confidence when it comes time to write your next appeal, but they don't do a good job of explaining who to send it to, or why, or what results you might expect.

This book is neither a textbook nor a collection of tips and checklists (though I've written one of *those*, too!). *Money by Mail* presents a point of view I might as well state clearly at the outset:

Successful direct mail fundraising has little to do with statistics or with letter-writing. It's a long-term process that requires intelligent planning and careful, consistent management.

To succeed in direct mail fundraising over the long term, it's essential to *distinguish between strategy and tactics*. As in any other field, you can win the battle and lose the war. In this book, I hope to help illuminate the difference.

In military usage, the distinction between a nation's strategy and tactics is straightforward:

■ *Strategy* is the manner in which a nation seeks to ensure its security in peacetime as well as war, employing large-scale, long-range planning and development to make the best possible use of *all* its resources.

■ *Tactics* are the choices made concerning the use and deployment of military forces in actual combat.

Since few appreciate this bold distinction, the word "strategy" is often confused with tactics. In this discussion, I mean to draw the line just as sharply as do the Joint Chiefs of Staff.

The *strategy* employed by a nonprofit organization includes decisions about its leadership and policy priorities as well as resource development—not a plan but a vision. To set strategy is *not* to engage in "long-term planning" to determine how existing resources may be put to the best possible use. Setting strategy means dreaming about what you want your organization to accomplish. How to marshall the resources to reach that goal is an operational question—a matter of *tactics*.

Those tactics may include a direct mail fundraising program designed to help get you where you want to go, just as they may also include

lobbying, public relations, establishing fees for services, or merchandising.

I'm uncomfortable with this bellicose metaphor. I'd prefer to describe direct mail fundraising in terms of streams and rivers—or seeds that grow into trees, which cluster into groves and then over time become forests. "Strategy" and "tactics" smack of the nasty things I've spent many of my waking hours helping our clients stop. But I know of no other terms that help to draw so clear a distinction between decisions that are really important and those that aren't.

■ ■ ■ ■

For the sake of simplicity, this book assumes you're the executive director or chair of the board's fundraising committee of a nonprofit organization, or that you've recently been asked to take responsibility for your organization's fundraising as development director (or just plain "fundraiser"). But I also assume you know next to nothing about raising money.

It's possible that none of the examples cited in this book represents your type of nonprofit organization. But don't make the mistake of thinking an arts group can't learn from the experience of an educational institution or a civil rights organization. The differences matter a lot less than the similarities. What works well for a consumer group may also do the trick for a university, museum, or hospital. Many of the techniques of direct mail fundraising are broadly transferable. And from conversations with colleagues who raise money by mail in Canada and Australia, I know the same fundamental approach works elsewhere in the English-speaking world.

This book won't show you how to write, design, and mail an appeal for funds. Nor will it tell you how to think or plan or manage your organization. It will help you understand what direct mail can do for you.

My purpose in *Raising Money by Mail* is to explain and illustrate direct mail fundraising *in context*, as the means by which many nonprofit organizations have grown, increased their influence, and ensured their long-term financial stability.

Chances are, direct mail is one of the most effective tools your organization can use to prepare for the next century. But you can do so only with a creative, no-holds-barred, entrepreneurial approach to direct mail, making use of the newest insights and the latest technologies to gain maximum advantage for your organization.

I look on direct mail fundraising as a *business,* and you should, too. It's an entrepreneurial tool that can be used in a great many ways, for good or ill. Viewed narrowly as letter-writing or an occasional fund appeal, direct mail is unlikely to serve you well as the year 2000 draws near. But if you can make it serve the needs of your overall fundraising plan, it can help lay the foundation for your organization's continuing success well into the 21st Century.

■ ■ ■ ■

This book was originally titled *Revolution in the Mailbox* and published in 1990. It was successful far beyond my hopes. Reviewers actually agreed with my claim that the book met an important need! *Revolution in the Mailbox* was purchased by public libraries, by competing consulting firms for staff training programs, and by more than one thousand nonprofit organizations. It was adopted as a textbook in several college and graduate school courses in nonprofit management and direct marketing. And the National Society of Fund Raising Executives (NSFRE) added it to their recommended reading list (despite my refusal to accept their spelling of the word "fundraising").

In revising this book for publication in late 1994, nearly five years after its first appearance, I made many changes. Here are the ones you can see:

■ Added text in several chapters, reflecting the lessons of the last five years
■ Updated facts and statistics
■ Many new illustrations
■ Minor editorial changes
■ More readable format and typography

But the big change is in what you *won't* read in this book.

Revolution in the Mailbox was written for political as well as nonprofit fundraisers. By far the longest chapter in that book—nearly seventy pages long—was devoted to the Rev. Jesse Jackson's 1988 Presidential campaign. Included were full reproductions of seven of the direct mail packages my colleagues and I created for the campaign. If you want to study those packages

now, you'll have to find a copy of the original *Revolution in the Mailbox.* (Strathmoor Press still has a few left.) And there were references throughout the book to the challenges of political fundraising. Those are gone, too.

I've also cut the final chapter of the original book, "Fundraising for the 21st Century." That chapter emphasized the political impact of direct mail fundraising and the emerging technologies that I expected (and still expect) to extend its influence well past the millennium. Many of the references to new technologies look stale to me now. (Heck, I wrote a book less than a year ago called *Technology and the Future of Fundraising,* and *that* already looks a little out of date!) Dropping two chapters and refocusing on nonprofit fundraising made the new title necessary.

The result of all these changes is an up-to-date book that exclusively addresses the fundraising realities of the nonprofit sector. Since it's also shorter and more compact, *Raising Money by Mail* is much cheaper to produce. That means we're able to set the price much lower—$19.95 versus the original $65.00—so this book will be accessible to many more nonprofit organizations. And that pleases the democrat in me.

I know, from working with hundreds of nonprofits over the past fifteen years, that almost every not-for-profit cause, institution, or organization can benefit from this book. It doesn't matter whether you *think* you're involved in direct mail fundraising, or want to be. You raise money by mail—whether you call it an annual fund, a membership program, or nothing special at all. If you have individual donors, or want to have some, it's inevitable that you'll use the mail to communicate with them at least some of the time.

■ ■ ■ ■

Not all the terms used in this book—or the methods described—are universally accepted among direct mail fundraisers. My colleagues and I in Mal Warwick & Associates, Inc. (Berkeley, Calif.) cherish a view of ourselves as creative, and we've actually won awards and a lot of public attention in support of that view. While all of us in the business follow the same basic rules—and it's standard practice to copy successful techniques from each other—the particular approach to direct mail fundraising laid out in these pages is ours alone. Direct mail practitioners in other firms may not even recognize some of the terminology used here.

Much the same goes for my much briefer references to telephone fundraising. I'm also involved in that industry, as co-founder and board chair of The Progressive Group, Inc. (Hadley, Mass.). The language I use and the examples I cite relating to telephone fundraising are from the experience I've gained through The Progressive Group.

For an accurate picture of my biases and limitations, you should also know I am the founder and chairman of Response Management Technologies, Inc. (Berkeley, Calif.). RMT processes gifts and provides other "back-end" services to nonprofits, including "list maintenance," data processing, and laser-printing. This involvement helps explain why I favor specialized service bureaus over in-house donor management programs.

Some of the examples cited here are obviously hypothetical, while others are real. Every real-life case study described here is derived from the experience of Mal Warwick & Associates, Inc., and so are all of the direct mail packages pictured in the illustrations. Wherever I refer to "us" or "we," that's who I mean.

To avoid distractions and make the subject of direct mail fundraising as accessible as possible, I've chosen not to use footnotes either to note parenthetical points or to cite references for facts or quotes. My graduate school instructors may be very disappointed. But I operate under the assumption that if something's important enough to include in a book, it ought to be in the text.

Some of what follows may not be popular in the fundraising community. So be it. My reason for getting into this business in the first place was to change the world. A lot has happened in the ten years since I stopped licking stamps and bought my first computer. As a group, direct mail fundraising consultants have played a major role in many of those events. We've helped nonprofit organizations meet urgent human needs, shape public opinion, and expand the boundaries of our culture. Direct mail has had a profound impact on American politics and society. But I think the world *still* needs changing.

Berkeley, California
September 1994

one

The strange new world of direct mail fundraising

The strategic uses of direct mail

FOR MANY NONPROFIT organizations, direct mail fundraising is a question of life or death. Often, it is strategically important simply because so much money is involved.

No one really knows how much American charities raise in a year, but the best available estimate for the year 1993 is that the figure topped $126 billion. This doesn't include some 20 billion hours of volunteer time contributed by 80 million Americans, which added an estimated value of $150 billion.

It's exceedingly difficult to determine how much of that money was contributed in response to appeals sent by mail. But, not long ago, after consulting postal officials, major mailers, statisticians, and econometricians—including several experts who had previously tried in vain to develop accurate estimates—I concluded that direct mail fundraising now yields an amount in the neighborhood of $30 billion per year.

Thirty *billion* dollars.

That's about one-half of one percent of the Gross National Product of the United States, or one out of every two hundred dollars generated by the largest economy in the world. That's *big* business by anyone's standards! And that's just one of the reasons nonprofit organizations can't afford to ignore or misunderstand direct mail fundraising.

While direct mail has become increasingly competitive, expensive, and difficult in recent years, other sources of charitable and public interest funding have also become harder to tap:

■ Grants from the federal government were sharply curtailed by the Reagan and Bush administrations, and the massive budget deficit offers little hope that President Clinton or future Presidents will be much more generous to nonprofits.

■ At best, foundations have always been reluctant to fund programs in perpetuity. Despite recent efforts to persuade foundation executives to grant funds for general support, most still want only to provide leadership gifts for pilot or demonstration projects. And seed grants for fundraising programs are the exception, not the rule.

■ Corporate giving rises and falls with frequent changes in tax laws and trends in corporate finance. The mergers and acquisitions characteristic of the 1980s have reduced—or entirely eliminated—many corporate philanthropic budgets.

■ Mushrooming sales of products and services by nonprofit enterprises have attracted unwelcome attention by the Internal Revenue Service and Congress, and statutory changes threaten this rich source of financial support for many organizations.

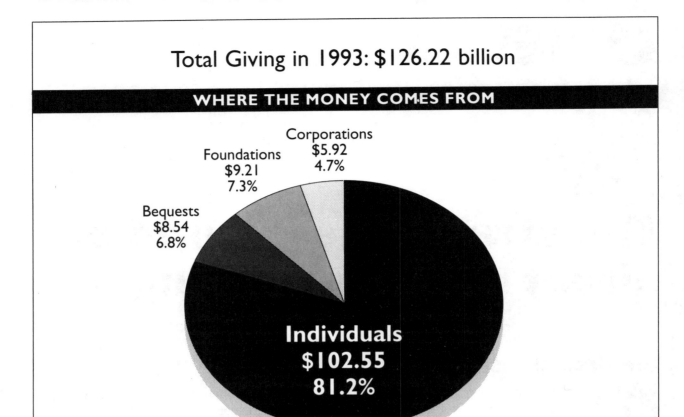

Total Giving in 1993: $126.22 billion

WHERE THE MONEY COMES FROM

Corporations
$5.92
4.7%

Foundations
$9.21
7.3%

Bequests
$8.54
6.8%

**Individuals
$102.55
81.2%**

Source: AAFRC Trust for Philanthropy

Individuals give five of every six charitable dollars.

By comparison, direct mail may be an extremely attractive option for your organization. It's the most widely employed technique to seek financial support from large numbers of *individuals*. Of an estimated $126 billion donated to American charities in 1993, more than $102 billion came from living individuals. Corporations contributed less than $6 billion, and foundations only a little over $9 billion. Even the remaining $8 billion in bequests originated from individuals. They were simply no longer alive.

Because of its ability to target, reach, and motivate individual people in large numbers, direct mail has come to occupy a significant place in our society and culture. Direct mail helps account for the vigor and broad scope of the so-called "Third Sector" or "Independent Sector"—that proliferation of seemingly countless voluntary associations in America about which De Tocqueville commented with such wonder more than 150 years ago.

There is no other country in which private citizens, working together in voluntary nongovernmental organizations, play such a vital role. U.S. nonprofits meet urgent human needs, train our young, enrich our culture, and help shape our public policy. They are one of the principal mechanisms in the larger system of checks and balances that guarantees the stability of American democracy.

The Internal Revenue Service reports that 530,592 tax-exempt organizations filed tax returns in 1993 showing income of $25,000 or more—but that's only part of the picture. There are well over *one million* nonprofit organizations in the United States (including roughly equal numbers of charities exempt from taxes under section 501(c)(3) of the Internal Revenue code and of other tax-exempt entities, chiefly churches). For the majority of these groups, direct mail fundraising is an indispensable tool.

Chances are your organization is already involved in direct mail fundraising. Even if you don't use direct mail to recruit or "acquire" donors, members, or subscribers, direct mail is probably an essential component of your overall development program. You may just call it something else.

Membership renewal notices, "annual appeals," newsletters, "special appeals," "action alerts," annual reports, "house mailings," "Letters from the Executive Director," "emergency appeals," subscription renewal notices—all these and many other possible forms of communication between you and your supporters play vital roles on the larger stage of your development program. It makes no difference at all whether you *call* them "direct mail."

Direct mail communications can help—or hinder—not only your fundraising efforts but all the work you do.

- Too many "emergency appeals" may undermine your credibility.
- Delays in sending dues renewal notices may cause your membership to shrink.
- Conflicting messages may confuse your clients or constituents.
- Failure to keep your supporters up-to-date through a newsletter may mean their response to your annual appeal will be poor.
- Multiple mailings of the same letter can anger even an ardent supporter.

To ensure that all these communications devices play a constructive role, it's important to take a close look at them *as a whole* in the context of your relationship with your constituency—and to consider how they all fit into your organization's strategy.

One thing is certain: your supporters will *expect* something in the mail from you. Mailing brings organizational credibility. Voters often tell campaign volunteers on the doorstep, "I'll just wait till I see something in the mail before I make up my mind." Your donors or members may be waiting, too.

Direct mail fundraising isn't just about money. Mail is often used to cultivate and recruit volunteers or prospects for fundraising dinners or other events. Direct mail is widely used for grassroots lobbying or other forms of political action by public policy groups and political campaigns. Schools, colleges, hospitals, and cultural institutions make wide use of direct mail to promote their community programs.

Direct mail is a flexible tool you can use to serve any one of a great number of organizational strategies. If direct mail fundraising works for your organization, it can take you down five divergent paths:

- *Growth*—by helping you build a bigger membership or list of contributors (called a "donor base")
- *Involvement*—by persuading your supporters to become actively involved
- *Efficiency*—by maximizing the net revenue you derive from your mailings, and thus raising funds at the lowest possible cost per dollar raised
- *Stability*—by reaching and maintaining an optimum level of direct mail fundraising activity
- *Visibility*—by publicizing your work among a particular constituency or the public in general

Later in this chapter, we'll take a look at several hypothetical case studies to explore some of these strategic paths and their tactical implications—that is, the specific forms of activity these contrasting approaches require. I hope that in that context the difference between strategy and tactics will become clearer. First, however, let's get down to the basics of direct mail fundraising so we can establish a common basis of understanding the issues.

What you can expect from direct mail

Direct mail is a difficult and expensive way to raise money. It requires capital investment, marketing skill, patience, and managerial agility.

Still, despite increased costs and ever fiercer competition for funds, direct mail fundraising remains the most effective way to build and cultivate a broad financial base. Over time, a properly managed direct mail fundraising program may be able to provide you with predictable, continuing support, year after year—and yield big dividends for your other fundraising programs as well.

But getting started in direct mail isn't easy. It's even harder if you have exaggerated or otherwise distorted expectations. I suggest the following as the first principle of direct mail fundraising:

Most of the time, almost no one will respond to your appeals for funds by mail. The only reason direct mail fundraising works is that someone who does send you a first gift is likely to send another when asked.

Direct mail fundraising is built on slim margins. Many mailings are regarded as very successful if just *one* in one hundred prospects responds with a gift. Of those who do respond, *ten* in one hundred may send their second gifts in response to a subsequent appeal.

The trick, then, is to identify your best prospective donors, to persuade the largest possible number of them to become first-time donors, to educate and motivate those newly acquired donors to give again and again, and to gain the maximum value from your committed donors by providing them with opportunities to support your organization ever more actively and generously.

Nowadays, for most organizations, acquiring new donors through the mail probably means *losing money* at least on the initial effort.

Nonprofit organizations have to expect to lose twenty to fifty percent of their investment in "prospecting" or "donor acquisition" programs carried out over time. That loss is sometimes even greater in the initial test mailing, which generally requires an up-front investment in creative and management services.

Despite the initial loss, this investment will help build your list of donors. However, it may be difficult for you to see all the way to the other end of that particular tunnel. I often feel that counseling clients to expand their prospecting efforts in the face of mounting losses is a lot like telling a child, "eat your vegetables." Prospecting is sometimes hard to swallow.

If you do, however, you'll see your list grow steadily over time and yield continuing dividends. Your newly acquired donors will, on average, remain donors for about two and one-half years. In that time, they'll typically make two or three additional gifts, averaging up to one and one-quarter times the size of their initial contri-

butions. Many will increase the frequency with which they give. They may also increase the size of their gifts. A very few will stay with you for life, loyally contributing year after year—and even go on giving after they die, by remembering you in their wills.

Perhaps most significant, among these newly acquired donors will be some individuals willing to contribute—or help raise—major gifts. For some organizations, a major gift can be as little as $100. For others, it may be $1 million or more. But the principle is the same: direct mail can help you identify, recruit, cultivate, and educate that small, vital group of prospective major donors who are capable of making a very big difference for your organization. There's no way to predict how many such donors will surface. But for a lot of nonprofit organizations the gifts from these major donors eventually provide fifty percent—and ultimately perhaps ninety percent or more—of total annual income.

■　■　■　■

It takes a lot of hard work to achieve this enormous potential. A successful direct mail fundraising program requires a carefully orchestrated schedule of additional mailings as well as telephone contact. Believe it or not, extensive research and testing have demonstrated that direct mail donors (a) really do like receiving mailings, (b) enjoy giving to lots of organizations, and (c) make repeated gifts to the groups that interest them the most.

In most cases, that means your most active donors should receive six or more fund appeals per year from your organization. Some groups mail twelve, sixteen, or even twenty solicitations per year—while also conducting telephone appeals and staging public events and other fundraising efforts. At the end of the calendar year, just before a major vote in Congress, or at some arbitrary program deadline, mail and telephone solicitations every seven to twelve *days* are not uncommon.

It's not difficult to understand why we mail so frequently. Most donors—especially direct mail donors—make contributions from *current* discretionary income. At any given time, they're likely to have only small amounts to spare. For all but the very rich or the very frugal, that's life in America today. Even those generous donors whose gifts to you may total more than $100 per year may be more comfortable sending several $50 checks than one much larger donation. They may even *think* of themselves as "$50 donors" and reflexively send checks in that amount to several organizations each month that inspire them to give—perhaps even without regard to whether they've recently given to any of them. Most direct mail donors write checks to charity when they're paying their bills on a weekly or monthly basis. Few people have large, fixed pools of money into which they dip for the funds to make small contributions. Even if they plan and schedule their charitable giving, they're likely to get the funds from their current income stream.

Few donors are aware how frequently they're solicited by mail. Again and again, surveys show that direct mail donors underestimate how many appeals they've received from a given organization. And while you may think that a majority is likely to complain about over-solicitation, most survey respondents say the frequency of appeals from organizations they support is "too little" or "just about right." Complaints much more commonly arise from individuals who *don't* support your organization.

Nonetheless, in a well-run direct mail fundraising program, you'll mail most of your appeals to only *some of* your donors. The key is to pick those who are most likely to respond, and to plan the most effective possible sequence and combination of solicitations.

Kind strangers and loving friends

There are distinctly different types of mailings to meet different fundraising needs. In the broadest terms, mailings are intended either *to acquire* new donors, members, or subscribers, or to *resolicit* previous donors for additional support. Between them is all the difference in the world.

It's the difference between the love of friends and the casual kindness of strangers.

"Donor acquisition"

"Donor acquisition" or "prospect" mailings— sometimes also called "cold mail"—are designed to persuade each potential donor to take the big step of giving you a first gift. While there are occasional and notable exceptions, acquisition mailings tend to be relatively inexpensive ($0.25 to $0.75 each) and are often produced in large quantities (50,000 to 1 million letters or more) and mailed relatively infrequently (perhaps two to six times per year). Acceptable "response rates"—the percentage of those who send gifts— are typically in the range of one-half to two and one-half percent.

Acquisition mailings almost always cost more money than the total of contributions received. In other words, they don't often break even. Their success or failure is generally evaluated in terms of *"donor acquisition cost,"* that is, the difference between the cost of the mailing and the amount it generated in contributions, divided by the number of donors acquired.

For example, if a $50,000 mailing generates proceeds of $40,000 and 2,500 new memberships, the acquisition cost is $4 per member ($50,000 less $40,000, or $10,000, divided by 2,500).

Donor acquisition and donor resolicitation mailings are normally different

The key is to calculate a donor's *value over time*—and keep the acquisition cost as far below it as your organizational strategy may dictate. (We'll go into that arithmetic in Chapter 5.)

The logic of this process is derived from the world of commercial direct mail. Based on the behavior of past subscribers, *Newsweek* knows how likely you are to renew your first-year subscription, and thus they know to the fraction of a cent how much additional revenue they can expect from you. L.L. Bean can guess to the penny how much additional merchandise you'll buy. Both *Newsweek* and L.L. Bean are willing to *pay* to persuade you to purchase a subscription or a woolen shirt. They're counting on the fact that sizable percentages of first-time customers will buy more of their goods. Those percentages are sizable enough that *Newsweek* and L. L. Bean will probably pay a lot *more* in direct mail costs than the revenue they receive from you. But don't shed any tears for them. Neither company is in any danger of going belly-up, because they make their profit in repeat sales that more than compensate them for the loss of acquiring new customers. Many large direct mail-based public interest organizations shrewdly apply similar rules in their donor acquisition programs.

For some organizations—sometimes for valid reasons, but usually not—*no* net loss in prospecting is acceptable. For others, the acceptable acquisition cost may range anywhere from $1 or $2 per donor to $25, $50, or more.

To achieve maximum economies of scale and help minimize your acquisition cost, you'll usually do best to develop *one* general donor acquisition package and remail it indefinitely in the largest possible quantities, so long as the package continues to produce acceptable results. While you'll be well advised to test alternative approaches at every opportunity, this standard, or "control," package will become the backbone of your donor acquisition program. Ideally, the control package is an "evergreen" appeal, theoretically good for all time. (For example, the control package for the *Wall Street Journal's* subscription promotion efforts as late as 1994 was reportedly first mailed in 1972—twenty-two years earlier! Just as examples abound in the world of commercial advertising of familiar, long-running campaigns, there are many other examples of durable direct mail control packages in fundraising for nonprofits.) Some large programs have several control packages, each targeting a different market, but the principle of standardization is much the same.

During the first year of a typical start-up program, acquisition letters greatly outnumber resolicitations. The following picture is common:

Month	ACQUISITION	RESOLICITATION
January	50,000	
February		
March		1,000
April	100,000	
May		
June		3,000
July		
August	150,000	
September		5,000
October		
November		6,000
December	300,000	
Total quantity	**600,000**	**15,000**

"Donor resolicitation"

By contrast, *"donor resolicitation"* or "donor renewal" mailings—often called "special appeals," "house appeals," or "house mailings"—have time-value and are usually written afresh for each appeal. In an aggressive direct mail fundraising program revolving around a donor list of 250,000 individuals, this might mean designing and writing as many as two or three *dozen* resolicitation packages per year. To achieve optimal impact, you're likely to invest more in renewal mailings ($0.40 to $5.00 each) and mail them selectively in smaller quantities, depending on the size of your donor list (3,000 to 300,000 letters). Response rates may range from three percent to thirty percent or more, but are typically between six percent and twelve percent when sent to active, current donors.

To sum up the broad differences between acquisition and resolicitation mailings:

	ACQUISITION	RESOLICITATION
Purpose	Build donor base	Net profit
Cost per piece	$0.25-0.75	$0.40-5.00
Quantity per mailing	50,000-1,000,000	3,000-300,000
Response rate	0.5%-2.5%	6%-12%

Persuading members to renew takes persistence

The annual "membership renewal" letter is a special type of resolicitation used by organizations with formal membership structures. If yours is a membership group, you'll probably mail a *series* of inexpensive renewal letters—as many as six or eight—with each member receiving as many letters as necessary to force the issue. In a typical renewal series spaced out over six to ten months, perhaps sixty percent of the membership will sign up for another year—roughly half of them in response to the very first effort, and a quarter in response to the second. The final effort in the series is calculated to recapture reluctant members at a cost at least as low as that of direct mail prospecting (the "acquisition cost").

But this renewal series is *not* the organization's only source of membership contributions. Well-managed membership groups *also* mail special appeals to their members—often no fewer than are mailed by groups without a formal membership structure.

EFFORT NUMBER	WEEKS BEFORE OR AFTER MEMBERSHIP LAPSES	ARGUMENT	TYPICAL RESPONSE RATE
1	12 weeks before	Renew early	25-30%
2	8 weeks before	Time to renew	12-15%
3	4 weeks before	Friendly reminder	6-8%
4	1 week before	Did you forget?	4-6%
5	4 weeks after	Last newsletter just mailed	2-3%
6	8 weeks after	What's the problem?	1-3%
7	12 weeks after	Telephone reminder	10-15%
TOTAL	24-WEEK CYCLE		60-80%

Overall plan for a representative membership renewal series.

While an aggressive fundraising program may include a donor resolicitation every month, it's unlikely that a large number of the donors on the "file" (computerese for "list") will receive every appeal. Through "segmentation" we carefully select subgroups of donors for each package and each mailing, to achieve optimal impact and increase the program's cost-effectiveness. (We'll discuss segmentation in detail in Chapter 5.)

We normally evaluate the success of renewal mailings in terms of *net revenue*. While there are different yardsticks to measure the net, we usually look at the ratio of revenue to cost, which tends to range between two-to-one and ten-to-one in all but the very largest programs. (In other words, the cost of a dollar raised will range from $0.10 to $0.50.) The ratio is likely to vary greatly with the segmentation chosen, since some subgroups tend to be far more responsive than others.

In short, then, the challenge you'll face as you set out to launch a direct mail fundraising program is to acquire as many new donors as possible at a donor acquisition cost that is consistent with your strategy—and to analyze, cultivate, and resolicit your donor-file so you'll derive the maximum benefit for your organization.

The approach you take to direct mail fundraising has to fit *your* organization's needs. Just

a Jaguar isn't the "best" car for someone whose greatest need is for high fuel mileage, someone's formula-driven approach to direct mail isn't necessarily right for your organization.

Strategy and tactics in direct mail

Now that we share a common vocabulary and framework of understanding about direct mail fundraising, let's take a look at how direct mail may be used as *a strategic tool*.

Through strategic planning, a nonprofit can identify its goals and priorities. Ideally, the organization's staff leadership and board will undertake a formal process, producing a written document that spells out its strategy and identifies the tactics to be used over a period of at least three years.

Despite the admonitions of outside consultants and bothersome board members, most nonprofit organizations don't adopt formal strategic plans. Nonetheless, even the most informal and inarticulate group needs to be clear about its long-term goals and know the difference between today and tomorrow. If you don't understand why you're in business and how you'll marshal available resources to serve your organization's

MONTH	MEMBERSHIP RENEWAL EFFORT NUMBER*	SPECIAL APPEAL NUMBER	DONOR ACQUISITION MAILING NUMBER
January		1	1
February			
March		2	
April	1		
May	2	3	2
June	3		
July	4	4	
August	5		3
September	6	5	
October	7		4
November		6	
December			
TOTAL NUMBER	7	6	4

Assumes annual membership renewal series unrelated to individual members' anniversary dates.

Representative three-track direct mail schedule.

ends, you've got much bigger problems than can be solved by starting a direct mail fundraising program.

Once your priorities are clear, however, you can use direct mail fundraising to help you achieve *growth, involvement, efficiency, stability,* or *visibility*—whichever one your strategy requires. Within the tactical context of your direct mail fundraising program, all five of these goals may be important, and several of them indispensable—but as *strategies,* they may be mutually exclusive. To understand the tradeoffs and conflicts among them as you plan your direct mail fundraising program, consider three hypothetical case studies.

Case Study One:
Strategy dictates tactics

Your strategic goal as executive director of a newly launched public policy organization is to reverse national policy on one highly controversial issue within five years. The issue isn't so explosive as abortion rights or flag-burning. Let's say you want to lower the cost of auto insurance. Lacking other means, the *strategy* you've elected to bring this about is to mobilize public opinion and lobby the U.S. Congress for changes in the law.

Your $500,000 budget is met by a few venturesome foundations and fewer than 500 individual donors. Clearly, you lack the funding you need to mount the massive public relations campaign that might turn the tide in your favor. But you do have enough money to launch an aggressive direct mail donor acquisition program. If initial response is good, you might build a broad grassroots base for change within five years—and ultimately generate the funds to support a professional media campaign that will change attitudes among the general public and in the Congress.

This strategy dictates a likely set of *tactics:*

■ A first-year investment of $150,000 or more in direct mail, with additional investment in the second year

■ A grassroots lobbying campaign that asks prospective as well as proven donors to become actively involved by signing petitions, mailing postcards to Congress, and the like (not to the exclusion of direct organizing and lobbying efforts but to supplement them)

■ Distinctive themes, logos, colors, and slogans consistently employed on all materials used in the five-year campaign

■ An active outreach effort to involve your donors in educating and recruiting additional supporters

While mailing millions of letters all across the country will enhance your visibility, it's no substitute for the public exposure that a well-executed advertising and public relations effort might obtain for you on nationwide television. However, without a sizable base and enough of a

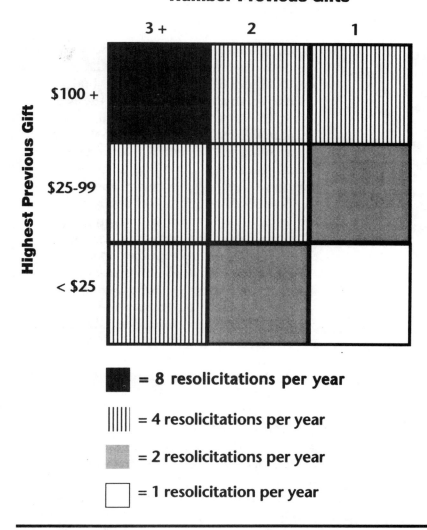

Stylized annual direct mail segmentation plan.

track record to gain the attention of skeptical reporters, your chances of free media coverage are slim. A massive direct mail base-building program is the fastest way to get there. Moreover, once you're there, the heightened public interest generated by national media coverage will boost your direct mail returns, perhaps dramatically.

To gain the maximum benefit from this approach, you'll reinvest all the proceeds of your direct mail program in additional and larger mailings for at least the first three years. Yes, this means that for three years every nickel of every direct mail contribution to your organization will be spent on mailing additional letters. These letters are the principal tool in service of your strategy, because they educate the public, involve thousands of people in active support of your cause, make you visible all across the country, and generate pressure directly on Congress.

If survey research and initial direct mail testing demonstrate substantial support for your goal of lowering auto insurance rates, this set of tactics will give you a real shot at achieving your strategic goal. But none of these tactics—not even the multimillion dollar prospecting program that is the centerpiece of the campaign—will be effective in isolation from the others. For example, without strong donor involvement and grassroots lobbying devices, the donor acquisition program will not support your *strategy* of bringing about a change in the law. All these tactics need to be seen in the larger context of organizational strategy—and executed as a whole.

To make the strategy work, you'll also have to *plan* the effort with great care. At the outset, numerical projections will be speculative and only marginally useful. But once results are in from successful initial tests, you'll be able to make meaningful projections. You'll be able to see—and plan—your five-year direct mail program as a continuous process, with growth targets established for each quarter-year along the way and a gradually quickening rhythm of activity in the final years that helps you reach your public policy goal.

Strategy often dictates tactics. In this case, a substantial initial investment in direct mail, aggressive donor acquisition, and reinvestment for rapid growth, and a multi-faceted program of donor involvement are all simply *tactical* tools to use in support of your strategy.

Case Study Two:
Tactics don't always work

You're the executive director of an agency that provides vital human services for a population of one million. The city where your principal office is located takes pride in its progressive tradition of providing for its least fortunate members. Your clients are disadvantaged teenagers. The *strategy* set by your board of trustees is to stabilize the agency's finances by broadening and diversifying your financial base.

Currently, your $1 million budget derives from fees for service, government and foundation funding, and the generous support of a handful of major donors, several of whom sit on the board. The agency has good media contacts and has managed to acquire a highly favorable reputation with the general public. While neither you nor your clients are front-page news, there's lots of drama and human interest in your work. You're convinced that direct mail will work well for you.

However, because some of your larger grants are to be phased out soon, your budget may shrink by as much as $500,000 over the next three years. You hope that a direct mail fundraising program will enable you to make up the loss, thus contributing ten percent of your annual budget within three years. Over the longer term, you hope it will yield a great deal more through collateral fundraising efforts such as planned giving, bequests, and other major donor programs. One of your funders has agreed to underwrite the effort to launch a direct mail program.

Among the *tactics* you've chosen to execute this diversification strategy are a public relations campaign to raise your agency's profile and an aggressive donor acquisition program. You hope to build an active direct mail base of some 30,000 people within three years, because you've been told that a fundraising program on that scale will generate net revenues of $500,000 per year.

That approach won't work. There simply aren't enough people living within the region you serve to sustain a direct mail program of such broad scope. Let's take a look at the numbers:

■ Because of donor "attrition" during the three-year period (through death, illness, address changes, or changing priorities), you'll have to acquire a total of perhaps 40,000 donors altogether.

- To acquire 40,000 donors, you'll probably need to mail 4 million prospect letters. Even with substantial reinforcement from a well-focused public relations campaign, a direct mail response rate of one percent would be quite respectable.
- In other words, you'll have to mail as many as 1 million letters in the first year and 1.5 million in each of the following two years. There are only 1 million people living in your region—and relatively few of them can be considered good prospects. (Later, after we've discussed mailing lists, you'll understand this statement better.)

To carry out this strategy, your agency will need to become a household word locally. In neighborhoods where your best prospects live, you'll need to persuade virtually every household to contribute to your work. This may be practical for a zoo or a museum with a creative community involvement program and lots of tangible membership benefits, but it's not in the cards for a social service agency.

Here, more realistically, are your options:

- Settle for a much smaller donor base, and a much more modest contribution to your operating budget. Direct mail probably will work for your agency. It just won't live up to unrealistic expectations.
- Forego profits entirely for three years—or even longer—as you reinvest them in donor acquisition and continuing public relations efforts. Even so, you may need to wait a lot longer than three years before the program begins to make a significant contribution to your budget.
- Consider whether the implications of your work warrant mailing outside your region, perhaps even nationally.
- Look for other ways to supplement or substitute for direct mail donor acquisition. A broad-based program of neighborhood fundraising events may be feasible. So might a multimedia campaign to generate "inquiries" about your services from individuals who write or call in response to your offer to tell them "how you can help." Direct mail appeals may succeed with these "qualified prospects" who have demonstrated interest in your work.

However, despite your best efforts, it's possible that direct mail will never generate net revenues of $500,000 per year for you.

Strategy may dictate tactics—but the tactics must be realistic.

Case Study Three: Tactics affect strategy

The challenge you face as chief executive officer of a nationwide advocacy group is to maintain your large membership base—essential for your ongoing lobbying campaign—while increasing your operating budget by at least twenty percent annually over the next four years. The environmental issues your group addresses are of increasing concern to the general public, and your board is confident there is lots of room for you to grow.

The *strategy* you've successfully pursued for three years already is to publish and promote by direct mail a lush, four-color monthly magazine which is available to members only. Repeated testing has shown that, by highlighting this attractive membership benefit, you can mail 5 million prospect letters per year and acquire 40,000 new members at break-even with entry-level dues set at $12. But there's a catch.

It costs you another $10 per year to print and mail the magazine to each member, and the typical $12 member doesn't respond well to appeals for additional gifts. The upshot is that your membership program as a whole isn't operating at much better than break-even. It's netting just enough to cover publication, distribution and overhead costs—with no significant net income to fund that twenty percent budgetary growth essential to your strategy.

One *tactical* solution to this dilemma is to raise your membership dues—in effect, your subscription price—to $15, $18, $20, or $25 (with testing to determine the optimal level). While the cost of fulfilling each individual magazine subscription will rise as circulation falls (because of reduced economies of scale), in all likelihood you'll be able to find a level of prospecting where you can continue to acquire new members at break-even while taking those added costs into account.

If you *reduce* your prospecting volume, you'll acquire fewer new members, so your membership base will shrink. But the shrinkage may be limited if you don't encounter great resistance to the

DUES LEVEL	VOLUME MAILABLE AT BREAKEVEN	NUMBER NEW MEMBERS	MAGAZINE AND MEMBER SERVICE COSTS	SPECIAL APPEAL INCOME	OTHER INCOME FROM NEW MEMBERS	NET INCOME FROM NEW MEMBERS
$12	5,000,000	40,000	$400,000	$120,000	$280,000	0
$15	4,000,000	35,000	$375,000	$157,500	$280,000	$62,500
$18	3,000,000	30,000	$350,000	$189,000	$270,000	$109,000
$20	2,500,000	25,000	$325,000	$218,750	$250,000	$143,750
$25	1,500,000	15,000	$300,000	$180,000	$165,000	$45,000

Financial realities may determine membership dues.

higher dues level. And you'll be attracting members, who will almost certainly respond better to your requests for more generous gifts. Because repeated testing shows that donors who send larger gifts also contribute more frequently and tend to be more loyal, those who pay dues of $20 or $25 per year are much more likely to be responsive to "special appeals." You can then finance the desired budgetary growth from these appeals and from a beefed-up major gifts program. It's also possible that with lower prospecting volume and fewer members you'll be able to cut costs in your fulfillment and membership departments, achieving the same effect as revenue growth.

But there are flaws in this tactical approach. You'll be operating with a smaller base, which runs the risk of undercutting your lobbying campaign. You may also be forced to lay off staff. Either of these considerations may rule out cutbacks in your prospecting efforts.

Thus, the tactics required to execute a sound strategy may dictate other changes in the way you run your organization. Some of these—such as a membership base that shrinks too much, or major changes in staffing requirements—may have unintended and unfortunate consequences. Careful planning will help minimize the problems. But only a clear sense of strategic priorities will allow you to make decisions that are right for your organization.

■ ■ ■ ■

The most productive way I've found to view direct mail fundraising in the strategic planning process is as a method of *problem-solving*. Once you've identified the problem—too few members to give you clout on Capitol Hill; too little money to meet your clients' needs; too much unpredictability in your finances—you can devise a solution using direct mail techniques.

The trick, of course, is to figure out what the problem is.

■ In the first of these three case studies, the new public policy organization, is the central problem finding funds for a public relations campaign . . . or is it controlling the cost of auto insurance?

■ In the hypothetical case of the human service agency, what's more important: broadening the funding base in the long term . . . or supporting the budget in the short run?

■ For the environmental advocacy group, is it a higher priority to maintain a large membership base . . . or to maximize net income?

The answers to these questions are not obvious. There are sound arguments for either side—or for still different points of view. But it's absolutely essential these questions be resolved. Decisions need to be made, one way or another. Muddled priorities are a prescription for failure.

Designing an effective direct mail fundraising program is, first of all, a matter of distinguishing strategy from tactics. And for the program to achieve its goals, that distinction must be clear to everyone involved in its management. The difference between strategy and tactics should never be forgotten.

Direct mail's not for everyone

These days, what passes for conventional wisdom in direct mail fundraising is that your initial acquisition test mailing will be successful if it breaks even—in other words, if it yields enough in direct, immediate contributions to cover the full cost of the mailing. From this conventional point of view, your successful program will then proceed with a series of progressively larger donor acquisition mailings, breaking even all along the way, as you build an ever-bigger list of proven donors *at no net cost.*

While this is an unfairly optimistic picture of the recent experience of most small and medium-sized nonprofits—and of a great many large ones, too—direct mail fundraising may be hugely successful for them, anyway, if they can acquire donors at an acceptable cost and then profitably resolicit them. Even the most modest test results may lay the foundation for a fundraising program of enormous scale.

But before we drift off into never-never land with our eyeballs full of dollar signs, let's make sure we agree on something:

This test mailing you're launching is *really* a test.

Direct mail is a risky business. Maybe—just maybe—your test won't work.

Sometimes a direct mail fundraising program gets off to a slow start. It may take more than one test mailing to identify a successful marketing concept, or to find the right market. But for some organizations, the *cost* of direct mail fundraising may be out of proportion to its potential yield.

Remember, a direct mail donor prospecting program must deliver new donors at an advantageous acquisition cost. If it doesn't do that, you'd better head back to the drawing boards. Direct mail may not be right for you.

Quite apart from the possibility that your initial test mailing may be poorly conceived or badly executed, public response may be limited for one or more of the following reasons:

- There may not be a large enough number of people who agree that your organization fills an important need—or it may be difficult to find mailing lists on which their names and addresses appear.
- People may agree the work you're doing is important—but not *care* strongly enough to send money.
- The ever-fickle public may feel the need you're filling has passed—or simply that it isn't *urgent* enough to require immediate support.
- Organizations that operate on a small scale may have an especially difficult time launching the type of large direct mail fundraising programs I'm describing in these pages: those with annual budgets of less than $300,000, or with constituencies of fewer than 2,000,000 people. While there are important exceptions, for the most part the market for a local public interest group in all but the largest metropolitan areas may simply be too small to apply these techniques. Professionally managed direct mail fundraising is built on economies of scale.

The limited size of your constituency or market is only one of several sound reasons *not* to embark on a program of direct mail fundraising. Direct mail may not be a good bet for you, and it may not even make sense for you to launch an initial test if any of the following conditions apply:

- If you lack the necessary *capital* to invest in a test mailing.
- If your finances are fragile and you can't bear the *risk* of an unsuccessful test.
- If the *issues* involved in your work aren't specific, compelling, and of concern to a broad public.
- If you can't effectively distinguish your organization from others serving the same constituency by identifying something *dramatic* or unique about you or your work.
- If your mission and *strategy* are unclear, so that it would be difficult to package your programs for a wider public.

- If you're just starting out and lack the track record, name recognition, or credentials to establish your *credibility*.
- If you have neither sufficient staff nor an outside firm to ensure donors will get the *service* they need.
- If your organization isn't committed for the *long haul*.

Direct mail may also be wrong for your organization if you or other central figures such as key board members or top executives are unable to swallow the unconventional logic on which the whole system is based—a set of principles and mechanisms that prompt some people to think of direct mail as somehow "immoral."

Is direct mail immoral?

One memorable afternoon some years ago, in a walnut-paneled Wall Street boardroom, I sat at a massive conference table across from a prominent former Cabinet member, engaged in one of the more frustrating conversations of my direct mail career. I was visiting him with the founder of a public interest group that the man supported enthusiastically. We hoped he'd agree to become the honorary co-chair of an intensive donor acquisition campaign based on the results of an encouraging initial test mailing. After our lengthy presentation, here's the gist of what he said:

"Let me see if I understand this correctly. You want me to put my name on a letter asking people to send $25 checks to my favorite charity—so you can send out more letters?"

Some feel this question poses difficult ethical issues for nonprofit organizations. To address them, let's review a few of the basic realities of direct mail fundraising:
- A well-planned and creatively executed direct mail fundraising program will ultimately raise a good deal of money for an organization committed to direct mail as one component of a long-term development campaign. At the same time, the direct mail program will give thousands—perhaps hundreds of thousands—of people the opportunity to support a charity they might otherwise be unaware of.
- It's true that initial returns from a direct mail program will be plowed back into producing and mailing more fundraising letters. Over time, however, the funds reinvested in direct mail will be a small percentage of the money earned by the program—and the rest of the money will be available to pay for the activities the group was set up to accomplish. As the years go by, the initial investment in direct mail may come to seem minuscule by comparison with the dividends it produces.
- Every fundraising program costs money, and a certain percentage of the returns from every fundraising effort goes to cover its costs—whether it's a benefit event, a newsletter, a T-shirt, or a direct service. Because a direct mail program may require a large initial investment, continuing reinvestment and a long-term commitment, it appears that the bulk of the proceeds are simply used to generate more letters. If this were true, no nonprofit would continue its direct mail program. Obviously, to be useful, direct mail fundraising must raise money to fund the organization's operations.
- Furthermore, consider that direct mail donor acquisition is the most cost-effective—and sometimes the *only* feasible way—for a nonprofit to build a broad financial base, expand its operations, and ensure its long-term survival.

There are those who feel it isn't right to ask the public to give by mail unless the organization discloses fully how it will spend every penny raised through the mail. As I was told in that boardroom, "Those $25 checks aren't going to be used to meet anyone's human needs. They're going to pay for more letters! I say it's immoral unless we *tell* people that's what their contributions are going to be used for."

The underlying principle here seems to be that if a fundraising letter asks people to send money to "Save the Whales," the public has the right to assume that every dollar they send will go directly to that specific purpose. That's just silly. No office runs without overhead, and no nonprofit runs without fundraising. A portion of every dollar raised—in any manner—must go to pay rent, telephone bills, office staff, and, yes, even further fundraising. Why should direct mail be singled out for scrutiny? A direct mail fundraising program can't be reduced to a formula. Numbers can be misleading unless you're looking at the big picture, because the numbers change over time—sometimes very rapidly.

Singling out the costs of direct mail also tends to distort its wider effects. A direct mail fundraising program must be seen in context because it contributes in a great many ways to the overall effort. For example, gifts from major donors probably won't be counted in the proceeds of a direct mail fundraising program, even if the program first made them aware of the organization's work. Thus, public disclosure about the *direct* costs and benefits of the direct mail fundraising program will obscure rather than illuminate the reality.

And there are some other important considerations when thinking about public disclosure issues:

- If costs and benefits are to be spelled out, it should be in the context of the organization's finances as a whole, rather than taking the direct mail program out of context. Existing law already provides for financial disclosure to the public, since charities' tax returns are available through the Internal Revenue Service, and in many states their financial statements may be obtained through charities registration offices.
- Public disclosure of fundraising costs and proceeds is a very blunt weapon with which to attack the tiny minority of fraudulent charities and consultants. Invariably, overlapping boards of directors, sweetheart contracts, or demonstrably fraudulent claims in the fundraising programs of these organizations will provide a much easier route to the heart of the matter.
- Freedom of speech is another applicable principle here. In fact, the U.S. Supreme Court has rejected on the basis of First Amendment rights the most stringent disclosure and reporting requirements legislated by the states. This freedom, in turn, encourages innovation—which may be the nonprofit sector's greatest contribution to American society.

With all this said, let me make absolutely clear that I believe direct mail must always tell the truth. No reputable direct mail consulting firm will work for any organization they feel isn't delivering on its promises. Ultimately, I'm convinced, donors will *respond* more generously to the truth than to exaggerated or distorted claims.

Now let's take a look at an entirely different argument used to question the ethics of direct mail fundraising. It crops up in cocktail party conversations from time to time, and in donors' letters to some environmental organizations:

"You people are cutting down millions of trees to send out God-knows-how-many letters nobody wants to receive. You should be ashamed of yourselves!"

I confess I don't feel an overwhelming sense of shame in the face of this argument, but it does warrant a response. Quite apart from the fact that there are much worthier targets of ecological zeal—chiefly, lumber companies who devastate the land by clear-cutting forests—there are several reasons why the argument is off the mark:

- Direct mail is used by nonprofit organizations because it's cost-effective—that is, it consumes fewer resources than alternative methods of fundraising and communications. Many nonprofit organizations could not exist without large-scale direct mail fundraising programs. Others would need to curtail programs serving millions of Americans.
- There are just two ways for most organizations to communicate with their supporters: using paper, or using electronic means. Television, radio, fax, and the telephone may all have roles to play in a fundraising or donor communications program, but they're no substitute for letters. Until we become a paperless society (a prospect I think unlikely even in the 21st century!), nonprofits will have to go on using the mails to do their jobs. After all, no one's proposing to abolish the U. S. Postal Service to save trees.

■ Direct mail fundraising packages account for a very small portion of the paper output of the United States economy. I can't prove it, but my doodling on the back of an envelope suggests that *The New York Times* and the *Los Angeles Times* together use more paper than all the country's direct mail fundraisers combined. Their Sunday editions may weigh more than ten pounds apiece—and each has Sunday circulation topping one million.

Many direct mail fundraising specialists (myself included) are actively seeking ways to increase the use of recycled paper. But truly recycled paper is still not universally available, and sometimes it's more expensive. My firm and others work with printers and paper manufacturers to seek solutions to these and other difficult problems.

Now, let's take a look at the question of what is ethical and proper in fundraising by examining more closely the question about financial disclosure raised in that Wall Street boardroom confrontation. This will help us see some of the broader issues and understand better some of the strategic implications of embarking upon a large-scale direct mail program.

Fundraising ratios and other deceptions

Conventional wisdom holds that the best way to measure your organization's efficiency is to look at the percentage of your income spent on overhead and fundraising. The popular press, the charitable "watchdog" agencies, and our own ingrown instincts all tell us this is the right way to determine whether you're doing a good job of running your nonprofit organization. As the argument goes, if you spend more than ten or twenty cents to raise a dollar—a "fundraising ratio" of ten to twenty percent—then there must be something wrong with you.

Well, that's bunk.

The fundraising ratio is a meaningful measurement for America's biggest charities: the Salvation Army, the American Heart Association, UNICEF, Goodwill Industries, CARE, the American Cancer Society. All these groups are decades old, command instant name recognition, and have large development departments. They possess the talent and the resources to use every conceivable means to raise money and can make the most of every dollar spent on fundraising. Each of them raises more than $300 million per year. But applying the same simplistic criteria to young nonprofits with budgets a hundredth or a thousandth the size usually makes no sense at all.

In exceptional cases, where fraud or flagrant mismanagement is suspected, an extremely high fundraising ratio *may* be an early warning signal. An organization that's spending ninety-five cents to raise every dollar after three or four years of extensive direct mail promotion is clearly not worthy of donors' support. A closer look may reveal that the organization is promising a miraculous cancer cure and working out of a third-floor walkup and a post office box, and that the organization's founder and $90,000-a-year executive director is the brother-in-law and former employee of its direct mail consultant. But, while fraudulent charities have existed since a charitable impulse moved some far-sighted noble to give away the first shekel, they are uncommon today. It's a tragic mistake to hobble thousands of sincere and effective nonprofit organizations with rules designed to inhibit a few bad actors. Moreover, where fraud is likely, an unusually high fundraising ratio is probably just one of many grave and obvious problems.

If charitable donors were to limit their gifts to the handful of the nation's more than one million nonprofit tax-exempt organizations that meet these conventional criteria for nonprofit performance, charities would be few and far between. Groups springing up to meet new needs—or simply to keep the old agencies honest—would die as quickly as they were born. Because only an organization with a truly secure funding base can fulfill these extravagant regulatory fantasies.

When a few phone calls and a lunch meeting with a wealthy donor can produce a multimillion-dollar gift or bequest, fundraising costs are minimal when expressed as a percentage of the proceeds. Much the same goes for an organization with a large, loyal following of donors who can be counted on to renew their support year after year. In either case, the fundraising ratio is likely to be low.

But a small, less well-established group—or one just starting out to address a newly emerging need—is unlikely to be in a position to achieve the same results with such little effort. It may take several years of repeat giving and continuous cultivation before you can *count* on getting gifts from a donor.

Fundraising is hard work—and for *most* nonprofits, it's expensive, especially at the beginning.

Partly because so many so-called "authorities" keep beating the drum for the most restrictive definitions of acceptable fundraising practices, relatively few donors will give more than token sums to any but the best-established, blue-ribbon charities. To smaller and newer organizations, gifts are typically much less generous. And obtaining them can take a great deal of time and money. People tend not to trust what they don't know.

To show the contrast, let's look at two hypothetical nonprofit organizations:

Charity A

Founded thirty years ago, Charity "A" has an annual budget of $12 million, which it obtains in the following manner:

Trustees and major donors	$4,000,000
Bequests and planned giving programs	2,000,000
Income from endowment (established 15 years ago)	2,000,000
Foundation and corporate support	2,000,000
Direct mail and telephone fundraising (from 30,000 donors)	1,000,000
Sale and licensing of products and services	1,000,000
Total Income Budget	$12,000,000

Organization B

Founded three years ago, Organization "B" has a $2 million budget which it meets as follows:

Foundation support	$900,000
Direct mail and telephone fundraising (from 20,000 donors)	600,000
Trustees and major donors	400,000
Sale of products and services	100,000
Total Income Budget	$2,000,000

It's entirely possible that Charity "A" and Organization "B" could each be spending $1 million per year on fundraising and overhead. For "A," this represents one-twelfth of its budget, or *eight cents* on the dollar. For "B," $1 million is half its revenue, or *fifty cents* on the dollar—more than six times as high a fundraising cost as that of "A." Does that make "A" six times "better" than "B?"

Not on your life!

Leave aside for the moment the possibility that the $11 million "A" has left over to spend directly on its programs might just be going down the drain on misguided or irrelevant projects, getting socked away in fatter and fatter "reserve" funds, or even keeping a passel of unimaginative people at work in featherbedding jobs. After all, "B" could just as easily have misbegotten priorities or incompetent staff. Let's just look a little closer at the *income* side of the ledger. The contrast is dramatic:

- "B's" work with major donors is just beginning. It's had few opportunities to identify or cultivate major donors or to establish a program of planned giving and bequests, much less an endowment fund. These are "A's" *principal* sources of financial support, but they took years to develop.

- Nearly half of "B's" $2 million budget is contributed by foundations. For "A," which receives grants worth more than twice as much, foundation and corporate support is only one-sixth of its total funding. Most foundations—and particularly corporate philanthropies, which may have stockholders to worry about—favor name-brand charities. Money attracts money.

- With its name less well-established and its merchandising program in its infancy, "B's" income from licensing and sale of products is only a tenth as great as "A's." Name recognition usually takes time to establish, and familiarity sells products as well as programs.

The real measure of a nonprofit organization's effectiveness is the cost of the *results* it gains. By that yardstick, many nonprofits with enviable fundraising ratios are singularly ineffective when compared to some of the scrappy, innovative, grassroots organizations with which I'm familiar—ventures that rarely are able to raise a dollar for less than thirty-five or forty cents.

Another big contrast between Charity "A" and Organization "B" lies in their direct mail and telephone fundraising programs:

- For "A," raising money from 30,000 direct mail donors, a great many of them of long standing, is a very profitable proposition. To replace those five or six thousand lost by attrition each year requires little new investment in donor acquisition. The full cost of "A's" direct mail program may be no more than $250,000. An overall revenue-to-cost ratio of four- or even six-to-one is not at all unlikely in a mature program of this sort.

- "B's" fast-growth direct mail strategy looks a lot different. In its second year of aggressive donor acquisition, "B" might even be spending on direct mail *more* than the $600,000 it's raising.

- "A's" direct mail program obviously emphasizes the cultivation *and resolicitation* of loyal, long-term donors. For "B," direct mail and telemarketing are tools to meet a different—and more costly—challenge: to identify and *recruit new donors.*

How does Organization "B" get to be like Charity "A?" By doing precisely what it's doing: methodically building and cultivating its donor base year after year.

As you can see clearly in this example, direct mail is only *one* of a great many fundraising tools nonprofit organizations can employ in the service of their strategies to make the world a better place. In fact, for all but a handful of nonprofits, a large-scale direct mail program makes little sense in the absence of other fundraising efforts, especially on the high end of the donor scale. For example, "B's" expensive, fast-growth strategy will really start paying off only when its development program includes major gift opportunities such as "A's."

Nonprofit organizations spring into existence to fill unmet needs, to challenge old concepts, and to espouse new ideas. It's no accident that many groups have such a tough time raising funds. What they advocate is downright unpopular.

But even those organizations that meet universally acknowledged needs and altogether avoid controversy are likely to face an uphill battle getting their fundraising programs up to a level of efficiency that allows for a consistently low fundraising ratio and still provides for necessary growth.

To do so takes *time*. After people, issues, and money, time is the fourth dimension of fundraising. It's often unseen and rarely appreciated. But no fundraising program may be fairly evaluated without a full understanding of this most precious of commodities. Time's great value will become much clearer as we look at direct mail fundraising in greater detail in the chapters ahead.

two

Starting out

L ET'S BE OPTIMISTIC. We'll assume the chair of your board's finance committee hasn't vetoed your plan to explore direct mail fundraising. In fact, she's helped you persuade other board members and your senior staff that the great potential in direct mail is worth the risk and the investment—even if you have to wait for several years to enjoy the payoff.

You've budgeted the funds for a test mailing, obtained promises from board members of substantial additional capital if the test is successful, and contracted with a consultant, who will work with you to develop the test package, acquire mailing lists, and manage the testing effort on your behalf.

Now, let's make sure we see eye-to-eye on some of the basic terms and premises of direct mail fundraising.

What makes direct mail work—or fail

You, as the leader of your organization, are the most important ingredient in your direct mail program—not so much because of your management or marketing skills but because of the quality of your leadership. Over time, the perception people have of you and your work will account for at least half the credit (or blame) for the success or failure of your direct mail fundraising efforts.

Your organization's record and the credibility and power of your message; the ties of your work to issues of broad public concern; how much publicity you get, and how good it is—all these factors will help determine how well you do in the mails. But they're only half the story.

There are many other factors—ingredients you and your consultants can control—that will greatly influence the results of your efforts to raise money by mail. Together, these controllable factors are about equal in impact to the leadership, reputation, and programmatic assets you bring to the program. The half that's controllable can be broken down in the following way:

■ *List selection*—This is far and away the most important controllable ingredient of a successful direct mail fundraising program. Call it a quarter of the pie, or about as much as all the other controllable elements combined. The most brilliant appeal for the most dynamic and well-managed organization in the world won't work at all if mailed to the wrong people. The lists selected for your initial donor acquisition test mailing must accurately reflect a cross-section of your potential constituency or "market." They should be lists that have been proven responsive to similar appeals. To make the right list choices for your mailing, someone will have to put in a great deal of time and effort. It's difficult to spend too much time selecting the lists.

■ *The "offer"*—How we structure the "pitch"— what we ask for, and what we tell people they're going to get in return for their support—is the most important creative element in our work. Call it five percent of the pie. Every package needs to be built around a "marketing concept"—a simple, straightforward connection between the "offer" and the "market" or intended audience. Before we write a single word of copy, we spend as much time as necessary to find the right marketing concept, and frame it with the right offer. The right decisions at this stage of development can make copywriting easy and stack the odds in favor of a successful outcome.

■ *Copywriting*—The actual wording of a fundraising appeal is less important than it's cracked up to be. Typically, the copywriter is responsible for researching the project and the letter-signer, devising the marketing concept, framing the offer, and, in many cases, making major design and format suggestions as well. If all this is what is meant by "copywriting," the job is absolutely crucial. But the copywriter's *words* themselves may not account for more than ten percent of an appeal's success or failure. Many people insist that the letter is the single most important element in a direct mail package, and we put a great deal of effort into creating compelling fundraising letters. But there's more to writing a fundraising package than just creating the letter. We devote great care to the creation of the outer envelope, response device, and all other package elements.

Good direct mail copywriting ties together all these pieces with the marketing concept.

■ *Format*—The size, shape, and color of the envelope, the character of the inserts, the appearance and accuracy of the recipient's name and address, and the extent (or lack) of "personalization" may all have significant bearing on the results. ("Personalization" is a regrettably inelegant term that signifies the addressee's own name, address, or other known individual facts are printed somewhere in the package.) Making the right format choices—especially whether or not to personalize, and if so to what extent—accounts for about five percent of the total. All the components of a direct mail package must fit together smoothly into an effective, working whole. Above all, a direct mail package must be not only cost-effective but also *credible:* the form of the package needs to match its purpose. We use a very wide variety of formats, because every fundraising campaign is unique and requires a unique competitive edge.

■ *Design*—Once the format is set, the designer's skill can have equal influence on the outcome, or five percent of the total. Bad design can obscure or undercut the best of offers. There are a great many specialized techniques in the

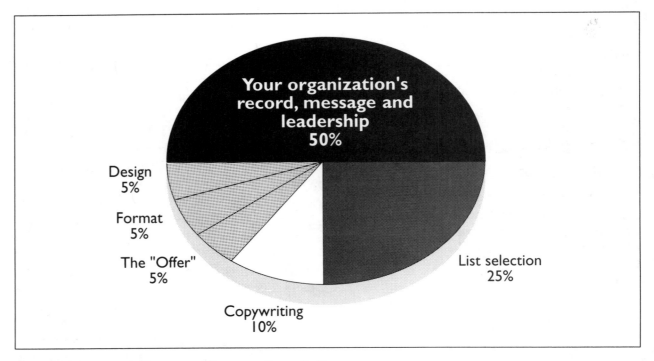

Many factors make a mailing work or fail.

direct mail design trade. After years of trial, error, and heartache—typically including brochures that are too big and envelopes too small—direct mail designers become superbly skilled at putting these techniques to work for their clients.

Now that all that's straight, you're ready to start. What's the first thing to do now?

Think. Because you're going to need a Big Idea.

Your marketing concept

The marketing concept is the Idea that pulls all the elements together—lists, offer, and signer—and ties them up with a bow. Direct mail fundraising is a form of marketing, and obtaining each individual contribution is a matter of closing a sale. Your "sales"—the monetary lifeblood of your organization—may sharply rise or fall as you succeed or fail in conceptualizing a marketing proposition that motivates your members, donors, or prospects. Keep this fundamental principle in mind:

Each of your mailings requires a unique marketing concept. Every mailing, and every marketing concept, must fit into an overall marketing strategy.

If it makes you uncomfortable to use the language of marketing, you might try another way of looking at the matter. Think instead about meeting donors' needs and solving their problems. Then your marketing concept might be thought of as the short form of a contract between you and your donors.

Your donors have to get something in return from you. While their motives for contributing to your work may seem to be uncomplicated altruism, the act of giving money reflects deeply held values and beliefs and responds to inner drives: for acceptance, for belonging, for feeling useful and effective, and for propagating their values and beliefs. These and other powerful impulses create expectations that are dangerous to ignore. Your marketing concept needs to address some of these deep-seated needs in an explicit and meaningful way.

A marketing concept won't work unless it can be expressed in a single paragraph. (You could squeeze it into one long-winded sentence—but why would you want to?)

To give you a sense of what I mean, here are four examples:

- "As one who appreciates the finer things in life, you will cherish for many years to come each magnificent issue of our bimonthly magazine on the visual arts. You'll receive the magazine free of charge as a Charter Member of the Museum with your gift of $45, $75, $150, or more. More importantly, however, you'll have the satisfaction of knowing your gift will help us showcase the exciting new work of emerging artists in our region."

- "Join thousands of other animal-lovers in America who are committed to stopping—once and for all—the shameful and shortsighted murder of sea mammals. Just display the free stickers I'm sending you, sign the enclosed Protest Petition, and send a tax-deductible gift of $25, $50, $100, or more to the Coalition."

- "As a former U.S. diplomat with firsthand experience in Third World hotspots, I am writing you and a few other distinguished Americans who have demonstrated a commitment to world peace. I ask you to join me as a Sponsor of the Institute's innovative new conflict-resolution program with a tax-deductible gift of $1,000."

- "Your renewal gift of as little as $25 will buy $50 or more worth of lumber and tools to help house America's homeless children. That's because your gift will be matched dollar for dollar by an anonymous donor through the Center's highly successful Matching Gift Program. You'll get double the satisfaction from your act of generosity."

Note that each of these marketing concepts makes clear *whom* we're writing, *what* we want from them, *why* we need money, and what we're *offering* in return. A fully developed marketing concept must include all four of these elements.

But I don't mean to suggest capsule statements like these would actually appear as is in any fundraising package. They're simply summaries of marketing concepts.

Envelope teasers may provoke curiosity.

In each of the four examples above, the organization has clarified precisely what it wants from the donor—a particular sum of money, and possibly other things as well—and what the donor will receive in return (although that may be implied or intangible). The marketing concept makes the connection between the signer of the appeal and the recipient, in recognition of the reality that the relationship will satisfy not only your organization's needs but the donor's needs as well.

Decide at the outset what you've got to "sell" and who you think will "buy" it. What you offer may be largely, or even exclusively, intangible, but even intangible benefits must be made explicit.

This task is akin to the fundamental challenge faced by any dynamic enterprise, whether nonprofit or commercial: figuring out what business you're really in. That may not be at all obvious. It may take considerable research and careful thought. But it's important you get it right.

Consider the four organizations cited in the foregoing examples:

■ In the eyes of the general public, and in budgetary terms, the Museum's principal activity— "the business it's in"—may actually be to publish a bimonthly magazine on the visual arts, despite the fact that the Museum's board may consider its mission to be showcasing young local artists. The marketing concept rightfully focuses on the magazine.

■ The Coalition's lobbying campaign about the murder of sea mammals may require more funds and more staff time than the public education program its strategic plan identifies as its primary mission. It may make more sense to say that the Coalition is in the business of influencing policymakers, not educating the general public. The Protest Petition highlighted in the marketing concept reflects this reality.

■ The Institute's "innovative new conflict-resolution program," envisioned as the centerpiece of its long-term strategy, may be less significant than its effort to recruit hundreds of prominent American citizens as Sponsors. The Institute may actually be in the business of organizing, lobbying, or public relations, not conflict resolution. It's appropriate that the marketing concept emphasize the many non-monetary contributions Sponsors make to the Institute.

- Because of its focus on the needs of homeless families, the housing construction program instituted by the Center may be less important than the social services provided by Center staff. Thus, the Center's marketing concept legitimately focuses on children and on donors' satisfaction at helping other people.

Unlike some other forms of advertising, direct mail fundraising is rarely subtle. When it is, its subtlety is simply and economically expressed. You have about eight seconds for the recipient to decide whether to open your appeal. Once she's opened it, you may have another minute or two to involve her in reading the letter and to begin answering her many skeptical questions. Unless you want to lose her from the outset, you'd better be prepared to hit her over the head with a simple, straightforward proposition that's clear from beginning to end. Your principal task is to *motivate* the recipients of your appeals to *act* in a particular way—to reach for their checkbooks, and right away. In such circumstances, subtlety rarely works.

Effective envelope "teaser" copy draws the recipient directly into the package in a straight line to the heart of the marketing concept. The very best direct mail packages reflect the marketing concept on every sheet of paper, from the outer envelope through the letter and supplementary enclosures to the "response device." Even the reply envelope won't escape unscathed if you think your concept all the way through from beginning to end. (In an emergency appeal, for example, you might print the name of the campaign or the word "RUSH" in the upper left-hand corner of the reply envelope—unless you could think of something original instead!)

If the "end" is a check that arrives in the mail, the "beginning" is the market itself: that group of individuals to whom you're mailing your letter. No direct mail marketing concept will work unless it's firmly grounded in an understanding of the list or lists you use.

The wonderful world of lists

In the 1994 edition of the mailing list catalog used most widely in the direct mail industry, there are entries for more than 25,000 lists. The catalog itself is three inches thick.

Yes, you got that right: 25,000 different mailing lists! It's a *big* business.

Lists are created because organizations keep on file the names of their members or supporters. Publications maintain lists of their subscribers. Government agencies keep records of license holders and taxpayers. Merchants and catalog merchandisers track their buyers. There are also companies in the business of compiling lists to rent or sell for a profit.

Individual lists vary in size from a few hundred names to more than 80 million. All told, there are *tens of billions* of names and addresses appearing in these readily available mailing lists. Most of the more than 250 million living Americans appear dozens of times, and so do quite a few who are dead. Many of us are included as individuals on literally hundreds of lists.

Mailing lists are by no means all alike. There are numerous ways to categorize or describe them, but in the context of direct mail fundraising, it's useful to group them into seven general types:

1. Donors— These people have contributed money, most likely in response to a direct mail fundraising appeal.

2. Members— They've paid membership dues to an organization, probably by mail.

3. Subscribers— These folks subscribe to a particular periodical. Many first did so in response to a direct mail subscription promotion.

4. Buyers— They've bought books or other goods by mail, in most cases through a catalog they received in the mail.

5. Inquiries and sweepstakes— These are individuals who have responded to an ad or a direct mail package with a request for information or a response to a survey or sweepstakes. They sent in little if any money.

6. "Compiled lists"— These are second-generation lists, produced by merging lists from different sources. For example, someone might compile a list of people who have joined or written letters of inquiry to many different organizations, perhaps dissimilar ones. Someone else's idea of a useful compiled list might be those individuals whose lifestyle or demographic characteristics—as revealed by such means as auto registrations or property tax rolls—fit a certain predetermined pattern. With rare exceptions, compiled lists do not consist of people whose principal shared characteristic is that they've contributed or spent money by mail.

7. "Good ideas"— These are the people on your board chair's Rolodex, or a list of your friends or neighbors, or the thousands of individuals to whom you've been sending your newsletter because somebody five years ago was just *sure* they would take any opportunity to support you. (They haven't, and they probably won't.)

There are thousands of available lists in each one of the first six of these categories. In a few cases, they're available directly from the "list owner." Hundreds of "list brokerage" firms manage the others, representing the owners to negotiate and manage the arrangements under which outsiders use their lists. It's a big industry, and list brokers tend to specialize not just in such broad-brush areas as "fundraising" but in narrowly defined fields such as liberal or conservative political lists, Catholic lists, or "New Age" lists. I don't hear very often about list brokers going out of business, so I assume they're doing well.

Through list brokers, you're able to gain access to the overwhelming majority of those 25,000 lists. Most are available on computer tapes in one or another of several standard formats that a direct mail service bureau is able to read. (Some lists are available only on mailing labels.)

The problem you face isn't getting hold of enough lists. It's figuring out which lists are likely to work for you.

Very few will. Only a handful of lists will be sure bets to work for your initial direct mail fundraising appeal. These so-called "hot" lists—including your own active supporters and generous, recent donors to organizations engaged in very similar work—are sometimes hard to come by. "Warm" lists are a little easier to obtain. These are the files which, based on experience with similar appeals, we feel are *likely* to be responsive enough to be cost-effective. But most lists are "cold." Only testing can tell whether they'll respond cost-effectively, and in most cases testing is a long shot. The overwhelming majority of cold lists, as far as you're concerned, might as well be printed with invisible ink. They simply won't work for your donor acquisition campaign, and you might as well forget about trying.

Choosing the right prospect lists is a demanding and sophisticated task. As a group, millionaires aren't good donor prospects for a group seeking to aid the homeless. Neither are people who are homeless. Just because the one group has money and the other has a direct interest in the issue is no guarantee either will respond to the appeal.

There's an ugly truth that applies even to your organization. Yes, yours is unquestionably the most exciting venture to come down the pike since the founding of the Smithsonian Institution. Even so, very *few people who are approached by mail will agree to support you*. That unpleasant fact—together with the limit on the money you're able to invest in direct mail donor acquisition—requires a very selective approach to the tens of thousands of available mailing lists.

To sift through all the possible lists for your initial prospect mailing we look at each list to evaluate the following elements:

- *Donor history*—The rule of thumb in our business is that "the people who give by mail are the people who give by mail." I've never heard a credible estimate of the percentage of the population that fits this category, but I suspect it's small—certainly a lot less than half, and probably less than a quarter of the American people. The best place to start looking for them is on *donor* lists.

- *"Mail-responsiveness"*—Generally, the best prospects are those who've developed the habit of using the postal system. That *doesn't* include everyone. Industry surveys suggest that only a little more than half of the American public will send money by mail for any reason whatsoever, other than to pay taxes, rent, or utility bills—and a great many people won't even do that. The Direct Marketing Association recently estimated that only fifty-five percent of the American public are mail-responsive and can thus presumably be found on lists of do-

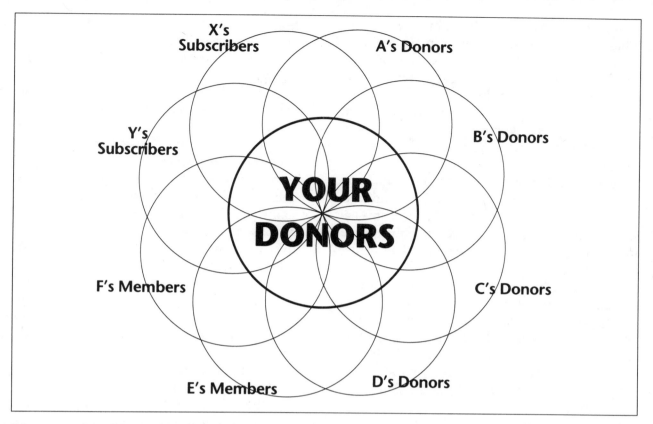

No organization commands its donors' exclusive loyalty.

ingly, the California Lottery Commission estimates that the same percentage of the adult population plays Lotto on a weekly basis.)

- *Recency*—One of the problems with most mailing lists is that they're not kept sufficiently up-to-date. In a society where one-fifth of the population moves every year, this can be a real problem. Generally speaking, only a mailing list that has been updated *within the past twelve months* is useful for fundraising purposes. A four- or five-year-old list may be worthless.

- *Accuracy*—A related problem for fundraisers is that the data entry on many publicly available mailing lists is atrocious. Some otherwise attractive lists may be poor prospects for your donor acquisition campaign simply because the list owner—or the computer service bureau that maintains the list—does such a consistently careless job. Among the most common and problematic errors are failure to record address changes and misspellings of names or addresses, both of which lead to high levels of undeliverable mail and to costly duplicate entries.

- *Affinity*—If your organization is building a children's hospital in Africa, donors to Save the Children or UNESCO might be a good bet for you to test in your donor acquisition campaign. The members of the National Rifle Association probably aren't. However, affinity is highly overrated and very limiting. The subscribers to a magazine specializing in international affairs could turn out to be your most responsive list of all. For one thing, that list may be far more accurate and up-to-date than most donor lists. Because it's so difficult to predict which lists will work, we do our best to find out which ones worked for similar appeals, thus taking the concept of affinity one step further.

The marketplace of lists

Most people seem to have the impression that mailing lists are bought and sold. In fact, this is only rarely the case. Lists are typically made available to direct mailers for *one-time use* only and may not be duplicated or re-used without explicit permission (which isn't often granted.)

Sometimes, lists are available on a *rental* basis. These days the going rate for most desirable donor and subscriber lists is in the range of seven to twelve cents per name ($70 to $120 per one thousand names). Some lists of "buyers" are even more costly. If you're forced to rely heavily on rentals, list costs may constitute one-sixth to one-third the entire cost of your donor acquisition mailing.

However, in many cases you'll be able to *exchange* lists and dramatically reduce this expenditure. Normally, exchanges are on a name- for-name basis. In other words, an exchange will obligate you to provide an equal number of equivalent names and addresses from your mailing list, usually weeks or months later. The cost of list exchanges is modest in comparison with list rentals.

The problem is, the owners of some lists which are available only on exchange may not be willing to trade with you. Unless you already have a sizable list of your own to prove your ability to reciprocate, you won't receive permission to use their lists.

If you're like most people I know, however, letting your organization's donor list out of your hands seems about as attractive as contracting a terminal illness. Here, then, is another reality you'll have to face at the outset: the business of direct mail fundraising is built in large part on (relatively) free commerce in lists, and those groups that lack desirable mailing lists or refuse to trade or rent their own are operating at a serious disadvantage.

There are three principal reasons some organizations advance to explain why they won't exchange or rent their lists. All lack substance.

- *First,* it's said that once a list is in the marketplace, it's vulnerable to theft. This is simple to combat. Like everyone else in the business, we insert what are termed "seed names" in each list we trade or rent. These are dummy names and addresses known only to us and not to the mailer who's getting our list. When the list is actually used, we receive "seed packages" at these dummy addresses. If packages turn up when they weren't supposed to, we take action. It almost never happens, and practical remedies are available if and when it does.
- A *second* objection often raised to justify withholding a donor list from the market is that it will allow other organizations to "steal" a

group's donors by making a more powerful and effective appeal. This reflects an unfortunate but common misunderstanding about fundraising realities: no organization "owns" its donors. All but the tiniest minority of donors contribute to a great many organizations, and certainly not just one. This is especially true of direct mail donors. Under some circumstances—such as when the timing of an appeal is inconvenient—it might make good sense to deny permission to competitive organizations to use your list. But most of the time it makes no sense at all. The truth is, a directly competitive organization probably has half a dozen other ways to reach your donors with its appeal through the periodicals they're likely to read or the areas where they live or the other groups to which they contribute. You might as well be neighborly about it and get something in return.

- The *third* reason frequently given to deny outside access to an organization's donor list is that the list will be "worn out" by overuse if other groups mail their appeals to it. My intuition tells me that there's some truth to this, and like some of my equally cautious colleagues in the industry I normally recommend that outside use of a list be limited to a maximum of one mailing per week—and avoided altogether during certain critical times on the fundraising calendar. But I honestly can't say I've ever seen any *evidence,* convincing or otherwise, that heavy outside usage of a donor list makes any difference whatsoever in the list owner's returns. There are even those who contend it's advantageous to allow others to appeal to your list, because it helps cultivate the habit of giving by mail!

Now let's plunge directly into planning your initial test mailing.

The initial test mailing

As the very first step in a planned campaign to establish a broad financial base for your organization, we normally conduct a donor acquisition or prospect *test* mailing. While the scope of initial tests varies from as few as 2,000 letters to as many as half a million, we typically begin with a mailing of between 30,000 and 100,000 packages. Usually, a test mailing will involve from one to three different fundraising letters, each with its own marketing concept.

The character and contents of the packages we mail may vary considerably, but they all share at least one common feature: some mechanism to identify each resulting gift by its *source*. To study the results of the mailing, we have to distinguish among the returns from different lists and from different package versions (if more than one is mailed).

In the past, this mechanism was usually a "Cheshire label"—a small rectangle of thin paper glued to the reply device or directly to the reply envelope. The Cheshire label, still common, serves double duty as a mailing label and as the bearer of a symbol or "keycode" identifying the package and the list that correspond to each response we receive. However, more commonly nowadays, the keycode, name, and address are all imprinted directly on the response device.

For example, the keycode "620218" might signify a response to the 18th list and the second of two packages in mailing number 62. Coding mechanisms of this sort allow us to *test* in what the more presumptuous direct mail specialists call a "rigorous, scientific" manner.

The *goal* of the initial test mailing is to determine your organization's potential to sustain a cost-effective, broad-based, direct mail prospecting program through which you can build a substantial list of responsive donors. The specific *objectives* are typically as follows:

1. To test at least six and perhaps as many as thirty lists from several different "markets" or constituencies for their potential to yield acceptable returns.

2. To produce donations over the first few months that recover a substantial portion of the cost of the test.

3. To generate hundreds of new donors, members, or subscribers.

4. Most important of all for the future of your direct mail fundraising program, to produce at least one marketing concept and package design that will be the basis for subsequent resolicitation and prospect mailings.

A typical initial test mailing at 1994 prices costs from $20,000 to $75,000 (including all production and mailing costs as well as the consultant's fees). To test 50,000 pieces of one package costs $25,000 to $35,000. Major cost variables include the number of different "packages" employed, the number of letters mailed, the consultant's fees, the quality of printing, the postage rate, and the technology used to print, address, and process the mailing.

It's always difficult, at best, to estimate the returns from an initial test mailing, but it's rarely prudent to assume it will recover more than two-thirds of its cost. We've frequently conducted *profitable* test mailings, but I'm always loath to predict that outcome from an initial test. When starting a direct mail fundraising program from scratch, the management and creative fees can constitute a substantial overhead and raise the unit cost of the initial mailing. What you spend on the test mailing constitutes an *investment* in the possibility of a long-term development program.

Ten to sixteen weeks normally elapse from the time you and your consultant agree to conduct an initial test mailing until the day it's in the mail. When bulk rate postage is used, the first returns are likely to arrive no sooner than ten days after the maildate, and it may be a total of three weeks before you receive *significant* returns. However, we usually prefer to wait for an additional three or four weeks of significant returns before drawing even preliminary conclusions about the effectiveness of the mailing, and to get a clear picture of the project—to draw conclusions about what lists might be included in a second, "continuation" mailing—we like to have a full eight to sixteen weeks of returns. In other words, a total of about five to eight months will elapse from the formal commitment to conduct a test mailing until the results are analyzed.

In some cases, the timetable for the initial test can be accelerated, and results made available much sooner, but that's not always advisable. Both creative development and list acquisition are complicated and time-consuming processes, often surprisingly so. Devising an effective marketing concept normally takes concentration and time. List brokers and computer service bureaus have timetables, procedures, and priorities of their own. So do printers and "lettershops" (where the individual components of your mailing will be collated, inserted, and packaged for the post office). It's risky to speed up the people who perform these vital services. Another of the ways corners can be cut with uncertain effect is to eliminate that step in the process which reduces the number of duplicate appeals.

What to do about duplicate appeals

At the outset, you may be able to avoid the issue of duplicate appeals. With initial test mailings of fewer than 50,000 names—some say 100,000—it's generally not recommended to take steps to reduce duplication. Sooner or later, though, the issue will catch up with you because your donors (or your trustees) write or call to complain, or because it dawns on you how much money you're losing by printing and mailing duplicates. For some organizations, this becomes an emotional issue of major proportions. It's wise to think through in advance how you'll handle it.

Let's assume you and the chair of your board's fundraising committee have the same visceral reaction to duplicates as I do: you *despise* them. You may also be convinced that enough of your potential supporters will be annoyed by receiving duplicate appeals that in the long run it will even be worthwhile to pay a little extra for the test mailing to cut down the number of duplicates.

Using a computer technique called a "merge-purge," it's possible to combine all the names in your mailing into one merged list, and then to identify and isolate the duplicates (called "multi-buyers," "multi-donors," or "merge dupes") so you can save money on printing and postage. However, it's not quite that simple.

For one thing, merge-purge is a costly procedure, running anywhere from a few tenths of a cent per name to as much as one and a half cents (or about $3 per thousand to $18 per thousand).

LIST	QUANTITY BEFORE MERGE-PURGE	UNIQUE NAMES AFTER MERGE-PURGE
1	5,000	3,800
2	5,000	3,900
3	5,000	4,000
4	5,000	4,100
5	5,000	4,200
6	5,000	4,300
7	5,000	4,500
8	5,000	4,600
9	4,000	3,100
10	4,000	3,300
11	4,000	3,500
12	4,000	3,700
Merge-Dupes		3,000
TOTAL	**56,000**	**50,000**

A merge-purge identifies and reduces duplicates.

In most situations, a merge-purge will save you money, but not always. In a 50,000-piece test mailing, you're unlikely to pay more than $700 for a merge-purge, but the cost may mount to thousands of dollars in larger acquisition mailings.

A merge-purge often adds days, and usually a week or longer, to the time needed to prepare a mailing. Like the added cost, this is a price that needs to be analyzed.

Merge-purge is a broad concept that refers to a range of techniques and approaches. Some merge-purge programs are permissively "loose"—allowing lots of possible duplicates to get through, for fear of cutting down on the number of good names to mail—and some are "tight." The difference can be considerable. Merge-purge programs sometimes also offer many optional features:

- Correcting bad ZIP codes
- Eliminating incomplete names and addresses
- Sorting names into order for postal "pre-sort" discounts
- Screening for surnames of particular ethnicity
- Affixing Congressional district or other geodemograhic information

The list of possible enhancements is long, and the implications for your direct mail program can be significant.

For an organization with a donor list of significant size, there is one overwhelming reason to conduct a merge-purge for every prospect mailing: it makes it possible to exclude most (though not all) of your own donors. Not doing so may be very costly. Some of your contributors will become mightily annoyed by receiving duplicate appeals, especially appeals that don't recognize the fact they've already given you money. More important, however, your prospect letter probably doesn't ask for a big enough gift and will give your donors a way to get off the hook with smaller gifts than they would send in response to a resolicitation. The difference can be considerable.

If you actually read a merge-purge report, you'll lose forever any remaining illusion that your donors are exclusively your own. The report for your initial test mailing may show ten, twenty, thirty, or even forty percent or more overlap among the lists you're testing. The rate of duplication will vary greatly from one list to another, but you're likely to find that the very

"best" lists—those that are most responsive to your appeals—are the ones that overlap the *most* with your own list (and with each other). Those that overlap the least—and are thus most dissimilar—tend to be less responsive.

In a typical 50,000-piece test mailing, you may find you'll need a total of 56,000 names, or an additional twelve percent, to produce the correct number of mailing labels.

Merging 56,000 names derived from, say, twelve different lists, the computer may identify approximately 47,000 as "unique" names. Most of the other 9,000 names duplicate some of the 47,000 unique names, and in some cases each other as well. Three thousand of the 9,000 merge-dupes match *just one* of the 47,000 names. These 3,000 will be formed into a list of their own.

Including the 47,000 unique names, this will make a total of 50,000 names "out of merge" on twelve original lists plus a list of merge-dupes. The other 6,000 names are either multiple duplicates (which appear on *three or* more lists) or bad addresses. In this case, all 6,000 names will be ignored.

The list of merge-dupes has a special function—one that helps to justify the cost and the time spent on the merge-purge. Since you've already paid for them at least twice (either in cash or in names to be exchanged), it's perfectly appropriate for you to *mail* to them twice. It's often profitable, since these are the names of those *most* likely to respond to your appeal. Some of these individuals are direct mail junkies who may contribute regularly to scores or even hundreds of organizations (and some are probably consultants like me who are reading everything the competition is sending out!). Chances are, you'll mail the merge-dupes three to six weeks following the main maildate of your test, and the list will likely perform at least as well as the average of the other twelve lists. Occasionally, it proves to be the *best of* them all.

In this hypothetical example of a 50,000-piece test mailing, the "merge factor" or "dupe rate"—the percentage of names identified as duplicates or bad addresses—was 16%. (That's 9,000 divided by 56,000.) In larger quantities, when you're mailing the full lists and not just small "test panels" of 5,000 names or so, that percentage will go *up*. (Don't ask me why. I'll blame it on statistics.)

In such cases, with high merge factors, the economics of merge-purge will be favorable for you. Your 50,000-piece test mailing will "save" you the cost of mailing to 6,000 multiple duplicates and bad addresses. If your cost in the mail is $350 per thousand, that's a savings of more than $2,000—far more than you'll pay for the merge-purge.

Now, you might argue you never had any intention of mailing to more than 50,000 individuals—but, the truth is, you're getting the *benefit* of mailing to 56,000. In larger quantities—if the merge factor is still high—the advantage might be even greater, since merge-purge costs fall more rapidly than most other mailing costs as quantities increase.

The merge-purge is just one of those many details that can make or break your direct mail fundraising program. Another is the nettlesome issue of who will sign your letter.

Choosing the right signer

For reasons that aren't entirely clear to me, at least one-third of the initial test mailings we've helped to launch over the years have been delayed—sometimes for more than *a year*—while the executive director or the board chair chased after the supposedly "perfect" signatory.

It's not worth the wait.

In fact, you should immediately rule out the following three persons as prospective signers for your direct mail donor acquisition letter:

1. That Hollywood star you cornered at somebody else's fundraiser, who told you then he'd really love to help you out.

2. The famous novelist who went to college with the chair of your board and who could probably help punch up the letter a little bit, too (and maybe even write it herself).

3. That college professor who's a world-renowned expert in the issue your group is addressing and is well known to all forty-five people in his field.

The "famous" novelist, actor, or expert may have the name recognition to get an envelope opened—but will anyone be convinced she knows what she's talking about? Is she genuinely involved in your issue, and preferably in your organization as a long-time board member or volunteer? Is her image such that she'll be taken seriously? What will she say if someone asks her a question about you on a TV talk show? And is she really widely known among the general public and not just to a narrow audience? Name recognition is easily overestimated, and it may not last.

For a successful direct mail fundraising program, the person who signs your appeal needs to be prepared for the long haul, too. Does she understand that if the letter works well, you need to mail it again and again to achieve economies of scale? Or will she inform you after you've printed her name on 250,000 envelopes for the next mailing that she's decided not to allow you to use her name anymore?

Now, how about copy approval? Is that Hollywood star of yours available to review the draft of the letter—or is he on location ninety miles outside Tashkent for the next four months and reachable only by camel train? Will his agent, manager, or secretary actually show him your letter? Once the copy reaches him, will he declare dogmatically that he won't sign anything longer than one page? Will he insist on rewriting the letter because it doesn't fit his image to ask directly for money? Will he refuse to allow you to include any references to his own, relevant experiences because "that's too personal"? Will he sit indecisively on the text without responding to your phone calls, while the maildate for your test slips ever farther into the dim recesses of the future?

Lest these problems sound farfetched, I hereby affirm that I've encountered every single one of them at least once—and in some cases five or six times—within the past ten years. This experience has helped lead me to a conclusion you may find perplexing: As the executive director of your organization, you are probably the very best signatory for your donor acquisition letter.

After all, who can more credibly tell your story than you?

A famous name alone is no guarantee of good response for a direct mail appeal. Time and again, I've seen appeals signed by Hollywood stars or celebrated authors outclassed by comparable letters mailed over the signatures of unknown, unsung staff or board members.

The key is *credibility*.

If someone else can tell your story more credibly than you—someone with good name recognition to boot—you may be well advised to take a back seat. If you do, just be sure the signatory you've selected has really bought into the process and won't cause more trouble than she's worth.

And lest you're tempted, out of insecurity, a need to compromise, or other motives, to *co-sign* your letter with a second person who will lend added authority to the appeal, keep this in mind:

A direct mail fundraising appeal is not a manifesto. It's a one-to-one communication—a letter from one person to another.

A direct mail letter needs to be written in the first person singular and addressed in the second person singular. Its success requires an emotional bond between the two. Only one person can sign a fundraising letter.

Whatever *individual* can write most convincingly and emotionally about your work is the best person to sign your appeal.

The best time to mail your appeal

"The best time to mail your appeal is when you've got it printed and there's enough postage in your account."

When my direct mail mentor gave that answer to an earnest question I'd asked about seasonal influences on direct mail fundraising, I didn't know whether to be puzzled or annoyed. Then came five or six years during which I watched appeals be delayed by red tape, procrastination, reluctant funders, screw-ups in the postal system, and computer crashes as well as arguments about seasonality. Finally, several dozen clients later, I understood at last:

If you're waiting for the perfect time to mail, your letters may never make it to the mailbox.

If there's any key to success in direct mail fundraising, it's this: *you have to mail, and mail, and mail some more.*

Yes, there *are* seasonal influences on direct mail fundraising, just as there are on just about every other form of marketing. An annual seasonality study conducted by a leading list brokerage firm showed that in 1993 an estimated 23 percent of all fundraising appeals went into the mails in November, while 13 percent were mailed in October and 9 percent in August. But those figures have changed greatly over time, according to the same study. Our own testing suggests that the patterns of seasonality will be different for your organization than they are for others. And unless you've got a huge budget for testing—or your organization is a chapter of a well-funded national nonprofit—you may never be able to afford the research needed to determine the seasonal patterns that bear on your particular direct mail program.

Besides: you can't possibly mail only during what you think is the "best time."

Some groups limit their prospecting efforts to one or two large mailings per year, presumably in the most favorable months. With sufficient capital, that may well be their very best donor acquisition strategy.

Resolicitations, however, are another matter altogether: donor resolicitation is a year-round process. As much as forty percent of all the funds contributed by mail are donated within the final quarter of the calendar year. For most—not all—nonprofit organizations, November and December are the "best" times to seek renewal gifts.

But the most successful year-end appeal won't come close to making up the revenue lost by failing to resolicit your donors during the other ten months of the year.

Keep in mind, too, that a month that's dead time for one group's fundraising program may be fruitful for another's. We've often found that mailing during months that are generally avoided by large, established charities produces better results for organizations that are less well known. Not everyone can compete with the Sierra Club or the Salvation Army—and you might be unwise to try.

Now, please join me in a look at the typical contents of a direct mail fundraising package—and at some of the issues commonly raised about them.

three

Anatomy of a direct mail fundraising package

IN THIS CHAPTER, I'll show you in pictures and words the individual components of a typical direct mail fundraising package. But keep in mind as you examine each of the elements portrayed in this chapter that there is no "best" or "perfect" example of any one of them. Every item in a successful direct mail fundraising package is a part of a *whole*—unified by a marketing concept.

As you'll see, putting together a direct mail fundraising package is not simply a matter of writing a letter and wrapping it up. In fact, the letter is often the *last* element I write. Rather, the entire package must reflect a clearly thought-out marketing concept. Once that is fixed, in your mind and on paper, you can start with any element of the package. In most cases, I begin with the reply device, which encapsulates the marketing concept.

All the pieces in a direct mail package must fit together neatly or they'll confuse rather than motivate. They'll prompt a response only if you've carefully thought through your marketing concept before you start to write.

The outer envelope, which gives donors or prospects their first look at your package, bears special consideration. The outer may require a lot of work—perhaps a third or more of the time allotted to copywriting and design, especially in the case of an acquisition package.

An especially clever or provocative "teaser" calculated to entice prospects to open the enve-

lope may be the hardest thing of all to write. But the very biggest challenge is to write outer envelope copy that's fully consistent with everything *inside* the envelope and leads recipients directly into the marketing concept.

Many fundraisers consider the outer (or carrier) envelope the most important element in a direct mail package.

The outer envelope

Outer envelopes, otherwise called "carrier envelopes" or simply "carriers" or "outers," come in a bewildering profusion of shapes, sizes, and colors. Occasionally, direct mail fundraising appeals are packaged without envelopes, in the form of self-mailing brochures or magazines or in such nontraditional formats as "card decks" (which are just about what they sound like they are). But most fundraisers keep coming back to the boring old technique of inserting letters in envelopes. Why? Because, almost all the time, it *works* better than other formats.

Direct mail designers, copywriters, and envelope manufacturers wrack their brains for ever new and more unusual wrappings, in relentless pursuit of the envelope to end all envelopes: one that *everyone* will open. But reality intrudes. Through our research, we've learned that, despite all these clever machinations to capture their attention, what people really look at first is *how their names and addresses are spelled!*

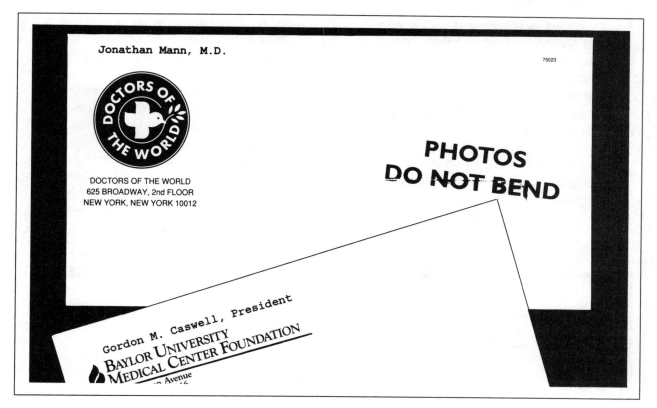

Postage

In its inscrutable wisdom, Congress requires the U.S. Postal Service to offer a wide variety of postal rates and delivery options. Although runaway inflation has reduced the advantage (and federal budget-cutting threatens to eliminate it entirely), comparatively low rates are still available to most nonprofit organizations.

The very cheapest rate applies to huge mailings "pre-sorted" into bundles for individual letter carriers, but discounts are also available on first-class postage if you pre-sort.

There are also several format options: stamps, metered postage, and pre-printed postal "indicia." Choosing among them may not be a trivial matter, because any one might significantly affect a mailing's results. But there may also be at least a slight difference in cost. For example, lettershops normally charge extra to affix stamps.

It's tempting to use the least expensive postage—but here's another one of those counterintuitive aspects of direct mail: the opposite is often true. We make extensive use of first-class postage—because it gets there faster and more reliably, because it's forwardable, because it gets more envelopes opened, and, most of all, because research often shows that first-class postage is more *cost-effective* than cheaper postal rates.

Ultimately, you may get just what you pay for, even when you're buying it from the U. S. Postal Service.

The letter

If I've heard it once, I've heard it ten thousand times: "Why insist on sending out these godawful four-page letters? I never write such long letters, and I'm sure I'd never *read* them!" Well, let's review the facts:

By testing this proposition again and again, we know that, almost all the time, longer letters generate more donations than shorter ones.

Studies show that lots of people actually do read four-page fundraising letters—in fact, many people even *like* getting them.

This continues to be true even now, after years of overflowing mailboxes, and even though *you* may automatically throw them into the trash. Ultimately, direct mail fundraising doesn't work on theory or intuition but on empirical fact.

Fundraising letters are almost as varied as the envelopes they're mailed in. But they're not much like business or personal letters, or even like advertising copy. Direct mail fundraising follows rules and rhythms of its own.

A successful appeal letter is likely to include five essential ingredients:

■ It establishes a one-on-one *linkage* or identification between the letter-signer and the individual person to whom the letter is addressed.

■ It presents an *offer* of an opportunity to participate in your organization (as a subscriber or member, for example, or by supporting some particular program).

■ It makes a compelling *case for* the offer.

■ It establishes *urgency*.

■ And it *asks* for a specific sum of money.

The reason most direct mail letters include these five ingredients is that testing proves fundraising appeals usually work better if they do. And that, in turn, is why they're typically long. It's often hard to tell enough of the story in just one or two pages to motivate a donor to *act*. To work well, a letter needs to make every reasonable argument for the donor to send money now, and

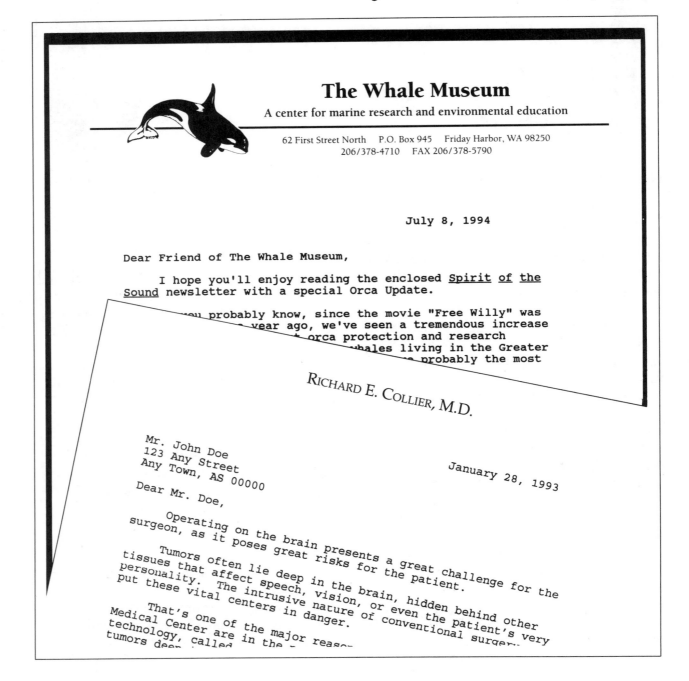

The Whale Museum

A center for marine research and environmental education

62 First Street North   P.O. Box 945   Friday Harbor, WA 98250
206/378-4710   FAX 206/378-5790

July 8, 1994

Dear Friend of The Whale Museum,

I hope you'll enjoy reading the enclosed <u>Spirit of the Sound</u> newsletter with a special Orca Update.

...ou probably know, since the movie "Free Willy" was
...year ago, we've seen a tremendous increase
...orca protection and research
...hales living in the Greater
...probably the most

RICHARD E. COLLIER, M.D.

Mr. John Doe
123 Any Street
Any Town, AS 00000

January 28, 1993

Dear Mr. Doe,

Operating on the brain presents a great challenge for the surgeon, as it poses great risks for the patient.

Tumors often lie deep in the brain, hidden behind other tissues that affect speech, vision, or even the patient's very personality. The intrusive nature of conventional surgery put these vital centers in danger.

That's one of the major reaso...
Medical Center are in the ...
technology, called ...
tumors deep...

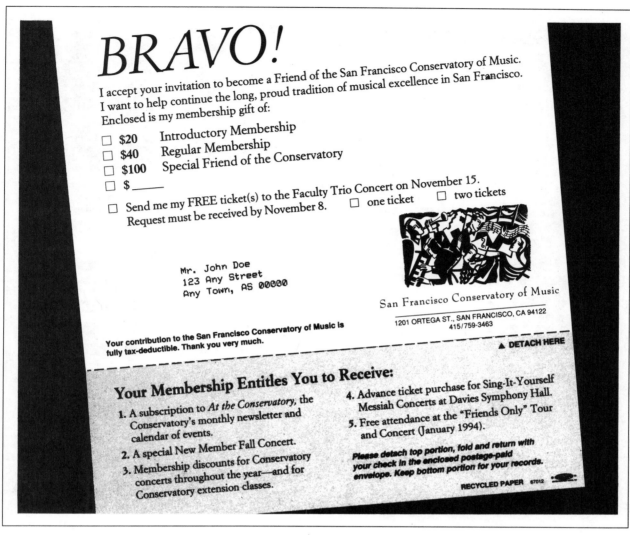

BRAVO!

I accept your invitation to become a Friend of the San Francisco Conservatory of Music. I want to help continue the long, proud tradition of musical excellence in San Francisco. Enclosed is my membership gift of:

- ☐ **$20** Introductory Membership
- ☐ **$40** Regular Membership
- ☐ **$100** Special Friend of the Conservatory
- ☐ **$____**

☐ Send me my FREE ticket(s) to the Faculty Trio Concert on November 15. Request must be received by November 8. ☐ one ticket ☐ two tickets

Mr. John Doe
123 Any Street
Any Town, AS 00000

San Francisco Conservatory of Music

1201 ORTEGA ST., SAN FRANCISCO, CA 94122
415/759-3463

Your contribution to the San Francisco Conservatory of Music is fully tax-deductible. Thank you very much.

▲ DETACH HERE

Your Membership Entitles You to Receive:

1. A subscription to *At the Conservatory,* the Conservatory's monthly newsletter and calendar of events.
2. A special New Member Fall Concert.
3. Membership discounts for Conservatory concerts throughout the year—and for Conservatory extension classes.
4. Advance ticket purchase for Sing-It-Yourself Messiah Concerts at Davies Symphony Hall.
5. Free attendance at the "Friends Only" Tour and Concert (January 1994).

Please detach top portion, fold and return with your check in the enclosed postage-paid envelope. Keep bottom portion for your records.

RECYCLED PAPER 67012

anticipate—and satisfy—every reasonable objection.

The reply device

A detached, stand-alone "reply device" or "response device" or "form" has repeatedly proven to be an indispensable element in fundraising packages, with only occasional exceptions.

For one thing, using a reply device is the most efficient way for you to obtain the donor's name and address, which normally appears on a label or direct imprint on the reply device.

But there's an even more important reason we include these devices. Studies prove that donors are more likely to respond if they're given something to *do* other than just write and return a check. If nothing else, they give donors a chance to correct the spelling of their names and addresses.

The reply device is the first thing most donors see when they open a fundraising package. Many donors set appeals aside, promising themselves they'll write checks later. They often keep reply devices but toss out the letters.

Many reply devices offer special opportunities for extra *involvement:* checking boxes, filling out surveys, signing petitions or the like. Response rates tend to rise the more such opportunities a package offers but the average gift often falls at the same time, since many of those who return petitions or surveys will send a dollar or two, presumably to help with "processing," instead of the larger sums the letter suggests. "Involvement devices" such as petitions usually aren't effective, however, when they're added gratuitously such as in a magazine sweepstakes offer. They work best when there's a credible link with the organization's strategy.

Sempervirens Fund
Drawer BE, Los Altos, California 94023

RECYCLED PAPER 89416

Verlyn Clausen
SEMPERVIRENS FUND
Drawer BE
Los Altos, CA 94023

NO POSTAGE
NECESSARY IF
MAILED IN THE
UNITED STATES

BUSINESS REPLY MAIL
FIRST CLASS MAIL PERMIT NO. 21975 SAN FRANCISCO, CA

POSTAGE WILL BE PAID BY ADDRESSEE

CALIFORNIA PACIFIC
MEDICAL CENTER FOUNDATION
P O BOX 7999
SAN FRANCISCO CA 94120-9648

The reply envelope

Direct mail fundraising works best when it's easy for a donor to respond. This almost always means an appeal will include a reply envelope—and most of the time it will be a "Business Reply Envelope" that the donor can mail postage-free without hunting for a stamp. (It will cost your organization at least $0.31 at current rates for the Postal Service to process each one.)

In many circumstances it makes sense to ask the donors to affix their own stamps. Some organizations obtain a higher response when they do. Other times, it's wise to put a "live stamp"—a real, live, first-class stamp—on the reply envelope. Only experience and testing can establish the appropriate approach for each mailing.

The brochure

For some reason (one that's always escaped me), most organizations want to include their general brochure in an initial direct mail fundraising test. This is rarely a good idea.

The marketing concept that is at the heart of a fundraising appeal needs to be tightly focused. Everything in the package should address that same focus. Even a brochure specifically designed and written for your direct mail package—one built on the same marketing concept—may not be much better than your general brochure.

More often than not, testing shows informational brochures *depress* rather than enhance response. They seem to distract donors from what we most want them to do: write a check.

"Front-end" premiums

Ask anyone in the advertising business to identify the most powerful word in the English language, and you're likely to be told it's "FREE." Wonder no more, then, why so many direct mail fundraising packages come with free stickers, decals, stamps, keychains, address labels, letter-openers, bumperstickers, and other such items.

These are so called "front-end" premiums, as opposed to "back-end" premiums, which are sent only in response to gifts from donors. The psychology established by these unsolicited free gifts is often not subtle. The operative mechanism is guilt. It's no accident that many donors send in a dollar or two in response. But there may be better reasons to use front-end premiums.

At their best, decals, stamps, and such can also be effective "involvement devices" that give donors something to do, reinforce the marketing concept, heighten your organization's visibility, and even play a role in educating the public.

Other enclosures

Some direct mail packages are fattened up with additional enclosures.

■ There are "lift letters" signed by celebrities or experts, normally brief and to the point.

■ There are "buckslips," usually small slips of paper that dramatically illustrate some attractive feature of the offer, such as a free calendar or book in return for gifts above a certain level, or highlight some up-to-the minute information about the organization's work.

■ There are news clippings, internal memoranda, budgets, and other supporting documents meant to strengthen the letter's case for supporting your organization.

Only methodical testing can establish when these items will improve the results. Often they don't.

You can help the New Forests Project intensify its environmental renewal and conservation efforts with the

Power of the Sun . . .

by becoming a Sponsor
1994 Spring/Summer S
Cooker Campaign . . .

Your FREE gift when you reactivate your Sojourners membership

▼ ▼ ▼

Crucible of Fire

The Church Confronts Apartheid

Orbis, softcover, 169 pages
$10.95 retail value

Sojourners' Editor Jim Wallis and Associate Editor Joyce Hollyday will send you a copy of their book, *Crucible of Fire: The Church Confronts Apartheid,* when we receive your membership renewal payment of $30 or more.

Through the words of South Africa's leading Christian figures in the anti-apartheid resistance, this book is an excellent case study in how faith and social action were brought together to affect significant historical change.

SOJOURNERS
2401 15th Street, N.W.
Washington, D.C. 20009

RECYCLED PAPER 21095

PHOTO © ALEXANDER LOWRY

Sempervirens Fund
For the preservation of redwood lands

four

Settling in for the long haul

THE IDEAL DIRECT MAIL prospecting program is one that attracts new donors at an *acceptable* acquisition cost. But what's "acceptable" to you?

Take my word for it: the break-even prospecting that may seem "acceptable" in the abstract could be impossible for you to attain. You could be making a big mistake to hold yourself to that standard simply because it seems "right." Building your donor base will mean a great deal to your organization. It may be worth paying a lot of money to keep your list growing.

Your challenge is to figure out *how much* it's worth.

In the next chapter, we'll examine several different methods for evaluating the worth of the donors you recruit through prospecting. You may then be able to apply specific numbers to your donor acquisition program, establishing criteria that relate uniquely to your organization's strategy and the role you've assigned to the direct mail program.

In this chapter, we'll look at the possibilities and the pitfalls of sustaining a direct mail fundraising program over the long term.

First, let's figure out whether it's worth trying.

Telling the difference between success and failure

You've finally gotten enough results from your initial test mailing to tell the story, and what they say is absolutely clear and unequivocal: *maybe* it's going to work.

- You've tested two slightly different versions of one package using samples from ten lists, splitting each of them down the middle. The total cost of this 50,000-piece test was $25,000. We project you'll receive a total of $12,500, and despite cautionary warnings, your Board of Directors had been expecting at least $20,000. From this initial test, you'll gain about 500 donors at an acquisition cost of $25 per donor—a level that's too high for your organization to sustain.

- Judging from the latest "flashcounts" (periodic list-by-list reports), one of the two package versions appears to be performing slightly better than the other. A statistical analyst who isn't too much of a purist would agree it's a better bet for the future. It might even produce results as much as twenty percent higher than the other one's—and we're all convinced in hindsight we could substantially boost the returns even more with several simple changes in the copy.

- Even with the better of the two existing packages, your mailing broke even on only three of the ten lists. Notably, however, two of those three are very large lists, with substantial potential for further mailing.

■ We project you'll be able to recover three-quarters of the costs and fees you might invest in a second, "continuation" (or "roll-out") mailing of 75,000 pieces. Our more favorable projections are based on three assumptions: (a) using the more successful of the two packages; (b) mailing to substantial numbers of new, yet unmailed names from the three most responsive lists; and (c) making what we believe are improvements in the copy.

■ The increased quantity and diminished start-up costs will also lower the mailing's unit cost. As a result, we expect you'll recover about $22,500 out of $30,000, gaining 900 new donors at a cost of $8.33 each. Because your capital is limited and your rudimentary fundraising program is unlikely to derive more than $20 in net revenue per donor per year, this acquisition

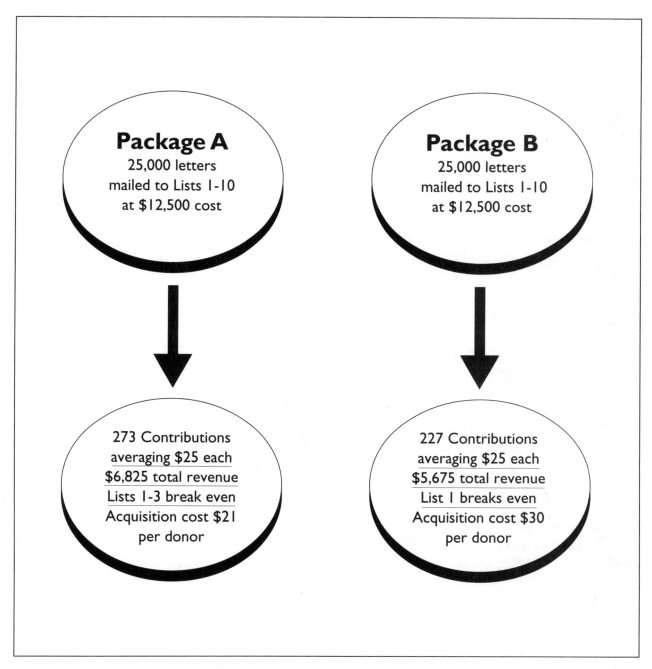

Package A
25,000 letters
mailed to Lists 1-10
at $12,500 cost

273 Contributions
averaging $25 each
$6,825 total revenue
Lists 1-3 break even
Acquisition cost $21
per donor

Package B
25,000 letters
mailed to Lists 1-10
at $12,500 cost

227 Contributions
averaging $25 each
$5,675 total revenue
List 1 breaks even
Acquisition cost $30
per donor

Mailing results often vary by package.

LIST	UNIVERSE	QUANTITY MAILED	GIFTS	REVENUE	PERCENT RESPONSE	AVERAGE GIFT	ACQUISITION COST/DONOR
LIST 1	100,000	5,000	120	$3,000	2.40%	$25	($4.17)
LIST 2	3,000	5,000	100	$2,650	2.00%	$27	($1.50)
LIST 3	250,000	5,000	88	$2,500	1.76%	$28	.00
LIST 4	4,000	5,000	55	$1,300	1.10%	$24	$21.82
LIST 5	450,000	5,000	50	$1,100	1.00%	$22	$28.00
LIST 6	10,000	5,000	40	$750	.80%	$19	$43.75
LIST 7	25,000	5,000	21	$603	.42%	$29	$90.33
LIST 8	50,000	5,000	12	$342	.24%	$29	$179.83
LIST 9	750,000	5,000	8	$155	.16%	$19	$293.13
LIST 10	1,500,000	5,000	6	$100	.12%	$17	$400.00
TOTAL		50,000	500	$12,500	1.00%	$25	$25.00
TEST PACKAGE A		25,000	273	$6,825	1.09%	$25	$20.79
TEST PACKAGE B		25,000	227	$5,675	0.91%	$25	$30.07

Periodic flashcounts show returns for each list mailed.

cost is much closer to the level your organization can sustain.

However, in a second mailing, we hope to learn enough from further list and package testing to lower that acquisition cost on subsequent mailings to the range of $3 to $5. Of course, there's no guarantee we can do so.

To proceed with a second mailing means either a fight with your board right now, or, possibly, a bigger conflict further down the line. What do you do?

The only way I know to deal with a problem of this sort—which is maddeningly common—is to decide *in advance* how to define a "successful" outcome for your direct mail test. There's no such thing as a workable universal definition, but here's a principle to start from:

The criteria that distinguish success from failure must be directly based on your organization's resources and strategic goals.

For some organizations, the scenario I've sketched above is very attractive. A well-capitalized group with an appealing action program and a handful of wealthy major donors might be nuts not to go ahead under these circumstances. So would one that's seeking to change prevailing attitudes on a matter of broad public policy and requires significant grassroots participation to do so.

Similarly, an organization committed to a long-range membership growth strategy—with sufficient capital on tap to make it work—might decide it's worth paying even $25 per donor. A $25 new-member acquisition cost could be well worthwhile for such an organization. (This figure corresponds, in the hypothetical case sketched out above, to returns of fifty cents on the dollar in prospecting.) The organization will recover its investment within less than a year, given generous returns from membership dues, special donor appeals, and collateral fundraising efforts that feed off the membership list.

By contrast, a narrowly based and underfunded effort to launch a new organization through the mails might wisely decide to leave the field with results like the above. The same goes for a well-established charity with a fully staffed development department. For a large organization, the case *against* direct mail in this scenario is even stronger if this, its first foray into direct mail donor acquisition, was a wistful effort to diversify its funding base.

More than once, I've seen half-hearted, compromised efforts at direct mail undertaken by cautious organizations. Board or staff members often end these experiments quickly. (Some groups are better off not trying.)

Every organization is unique. Your challenge is to make direct mail work uniquely for *you*.

Choosing lists for the next mailing

As you set out to select prospect lists for the second mailing in your donor acquisition campaign, you'll be forced once again to address those strategic considerations that determine the levels of investment and risk acceptable to your organization.

Let's assume we've identified fifteen possible lists to be used in your continuation mailing: Lists "A" through "O." They range in size ("universe") from 3,000 names to 250,000, with a total universe of one million names. Four months ago, you mailed to ten of them—"A" through "J"—so we can project the response rate and average contribution we anticipate from each of them. If we use all ten in your rollout, we'll be "re-mailing" four small lists, re-mailing portions of two others, and mailing to additional, yet untouched names on six lists. The other five lists—"K" through "O"—are to be newly tested, and it's anybody's guess what will happen when we mail to them. To be conservative, I've assumed poor results.

In the accompanying chart (see pages 52-53), I've ranked the fifteen lists from best-performing to worst, in terms of response rate. I've calculated the probable results of mailing to what appears from the test results to be the optimum quantity on each list. To simplify the picture, I've arbitrarily assumed we won't run a merge-purge.

For each list, the chart presents the mailing cost and anticipated gross and net returns, the projected number of new donors, and the acquisition cost for that list. (Costs vary from one list to another because some are available only as rentals and others only on exchange.) On the second column from the right, the chart shows on each row the *cumulative* profit or loss of mailing to all the lists down to and including the one on that row.

For the top five lists—"A" through "E"—we anticipate mailing to every available name. For most of the others, we'll select only a percentage of the names available. (To "roll out" to all the available names on a large list without repeated testing is a risky proposition.) This points to a total mailing quantity of up to 150,000 packages—only fifteen percent of the total number of names available on the fifteen lists. With lists that perform only moderately well at best, it's often unwise to "roll out" to the full universe.

In the long run, mailing to Lists "K" through "O"—the five "test" lists—may be the most significant aspect of this second mailing. Together, they constitute half the universe for the mailing as a whole. Each consists of at least 25,000 names. List "N" alone contains 250,000. To succeed with any of the five will make a meaningful contribution to the success of your direct mail program. Every prospect mailing should include list tests to explore new markets. You can and should mail more than once to those lists that constitute the core of your donor acquisition program because they work so very well. But there's a limit to remailing. List testing is never-ending.

On the final row of the chart you can see the total and cumulative impact of mailing all fifteen lists in the quantities indicated: a response rate of 1.6% and an average gift of $18. With a budget

LIST	UNIVERSE	QUANTITY	PCT RESPONSE	AVERAGE GIFT	GROSS INCOME
A	5,000	5,000	4.0%	$20	$4,000
B	10,000	10,000	3.5%	$18	6,300
C	3,000	3,000	3.0%	$18	1,620
D	15,000	15,000	2.5%	$16	6,000
E	5,000	5,000	2.0%	$18	1,800
F	75,000	25,000	1.8%	$20	8,750
G	150,000	25,000	1.5%	$18	6,750
H	25,000	12,000	1.3%	$16	2,400
I	5,000	5,000	1.0%	$14	700
J	200,000	20,000	.8%	$18	2,700
K	150,000	5,000	.8%	$16	600
L	25,000	5,000	.8%	$16	600
M	52,000	5,000	.8%	$16	600
N	250,000	5,000	.8%	$16	600
O	30,000	5,000	.8%	$16	600
	1,000,000	150,000	1.6%	$18	$44,020

Projected mailing results determine list selection.

of $65,000 and projected gross revenue of $44,020, the mailing is projected to lose $20,980, acquiring 2,465 new donors at an acquisition cost of $9 per donor.

Now here's where your strategy takes specific tactical shape:

- If your strategy requires you to *build your donor list* as quickly as possible and you've got the money to do so, your best tactical move is to mail all 150,000 names, and perhaps more besides. At an acquisition cost of $9, you may feel you're getting a bargain on nearly 2,500 new donors. Capital permitting, you might opt to mail 50,000 names or more on List "G," and all 25,000 names on List "H." If you're feeling really lucky, you might also test larger quantities on some of the new test lists.

- If, however, your strategy requires that you *conserve capital*—or if your cashflow is simply inadequate—you might mail only the top six or seven lists. Using Lists "A" through "F" will yield an estimated 1,553 new donors, and a net profit of $770. Mailing to 10,000 or 20,000 names on List "G" will eat up that profit, and more. But you'll still cut the projected loss in half, and the resulting acquisition cost for the mailing as a whole will be only about $5—a level you might well find acceptable.

- Nearly one-third, or $6,300, of the projected loss for the mailing as a whole will come from List "J," and more than one-half from Lists "J"

COST	NUMBER NEW DONORS	NET INCOME	CUMULATIVE INCOME	ACQUISITION COST
$2,000	200	$2,000	$2,000	($10)
4,500	350	1,800	3,800	(5)
1,200	90	420	4,220	(5)
6,750	375	(750)	3,470	2
2,000	100	(200)	3,270	2
11,250	438	(2,500)	770	6
11,250	375	(4,500)	(3,730)	12
4,800	150	(2,400)	(6,130)	16
2,000	50	(1,300)	(7,430)	26
9,000	150	(6,300)	(13,730)	42
2,000	38	(1,400)	(15,130)	37
2,000	38	(1,400)	(16,530)	37
2,000	38	(1,400)	(17,930)	37
2,250	38	(1,650)	(19,580)	44
2,000	38	(1,400)	(20,980)	37
$65,000	**2,465**	**($20,980)**	**($20,980)**	**$9**

and "G" combined. Those two lists, however, represent 350,000 prospective donors—more than one-third of the total universe for this mailing. If you're following a growth strategy—and particularly if workable large lists are few and far between for your program—you have to mail to these and other large lists despite painful losses.

We're projecting profits on only *three* of the fifteen individual lists. If you mail only to those three, you'll have a total of just 18,000 names available—too few to mail cost-effectively. The profits we project on Lists "A," "B," and "C" are significant only in that we expect them to cancel out the losses on Lists "D," "E," and "F." Even if you're cautious, you'll be well-advised to mail the largest possible quantity that will produce break-even results for the mailing *as a whole*.

You'll play out this process of prospect list selection again and again over the years. At every stage, your strategic goals will guide you. From time to time, cash flow considerations (or headline-grabbing events) may arbitrarily limit your freedom of action. But if they do so consistently, you'll need to reexamine your strategy and look for a way to capitalize your direct mail program.

The first three years

Let's assume you've chosen to take the plunge. You're going to proceed with a donor acquisition program, despite the equivocal results of your initial test. Assume, too, that your organization is new and underfunded. This is your first foray into the mails. You don't have either a large pool of capital or a significant existing donor list to underwrite an aggressive growth strategy.

For the sake of simplicity, I'll assume we received test results in the fall, and that your first-year program will get under way in January. The following table depicts your first year's mailing schedule and the increasing size of your donor list as the year unfolds:

Year One	Prospecting volume	Resolicitation volume	List size
January	75,000		500
February			1,500
March		1,350	1,500
April	125,000		1,500
May			3,250
June		3,000	3,250
July	150,000		3,250
August			5,350
September		4,750	5,350
October	150,000		5,350
November			7,350
December		6,500	7,350
Total	500,000	14,600	7,350

In the first year, we've mailed a little over half a million letters. The lion's share of the effort consisted of progressively larger donor acquisition mailings, one about every three months.

Through quarterly donor resolicitation mailings, we've netted enough to underwrite your investment in prospecting. (Note that not once have we resolicited all of the donors we've acquired. Some gave gifts so small they're unlikely to be cost-effective to ask for more. There are other, profitable uses for such names.)

If yours is a typical experience, you'll end the year at break-even after all of this activity, despite its unexciting beginning. Here, now, is what the second year's program might look like:

Year two	Prospecting volume	Resolicitation volume	List size
January	200,000		7,000
February		6,500	10,000
March			10,000
April	150,000	9,000	10,000
May			12,000
June		10,500	12,000
July	150,000		12,000
August		10,500	14,000
September			14,000
October	200,000	12,000	14,000
November			17,000
December		15,000	17,000
Total	700,000	60,500	17,000

By stepping up your donor acquisition program from 500,000 to 700,000 letters, we've added nearly 10,000 donors to your file. Meanwhile, we've increased the frequency of donor resolicitations from four in the first year to six in the second. Chances are, you've posted a *significant net profit* from direct mail this year. Your donor list has now reached a size at which resolicitation mailings are typically very cost-effective.

In the third year, your direct mail fundraising program may unfold as follows:

Year three	Prospecting volume	Resolicitation volume	List size
January	200,000		16,000
February		14,000	18,500
March		3,500	18,000
April	150,000	15,500	18,000
May			19,500
June		16,000	19,500
July	150,000		19,000
August		17,000	21,000
September			20,500
October	200,000	16,000	20,500
November		5,000	22,500
December		20,000	22,500
Total	700,000	107,000	22,500

By sustaining the same 700,000-piece-per-year rate of donor acquisition efforts, we've added another 10,000 names to your file in this third year.

However, the size of your donor base has grown only half that much, because we've been weeding out dead wood all along the way. We've dropped most of those first-year contributors who haven't sent checks since then, and we've taken extra pains to improve the accuracy of the file through address correction procedures.

Even so, we haven't mailed all the available active donor names in *any* of the eight resolicitation mailings. In six resolicitations, we've increased your net profits through careful segmentation based on individual donor histories. Also, both early and late in the year we've added small mailings that *target* only your most generous and responsive donors. (In the next chapter, we'll discuss the targeting issues that arise in resolicitation programs.)

In this third year, you've seen your investment—and your patience—really start paying off in a big way. The continuing cost of acquiring new donors represents only a fraction of the net proceeds of your increasingly frequent and selective donor resolicitation efforts.

And the donor base you've already built will continue paying off in a big way for many years to come.

Investment strategies: a banker's view of direct mail

Direct mail fundraising runs on two tracks: donor acquisition and donor resolicitation.

If you're starting from scratch, *acquiring donors* will dominate your attention for the first year (or two years, or even three, depending upon how much capital you have and how many risks you can take). As your list grows, however, *resoliciting* your donors will come to mean more and more to you. The profits from a single donor resolicitation mailing—just one of seven or ten you may conduct in your program's third year—could easily dwarf the net revenue from even a wildly successful initial test mailing, no matter how substantial it seemed at the time.

By the same token, those profits from resolicitation may make your initial losses from prospecting look downright puny.

To get a sense of how these factors play themselves out over time, let's take a look at two hypothetical examples.

Citizens For

Citizens For is not well-funded. The group started on a shoestring two years ago and only recently managed to beg, borrow, and steal $25,000 for an initial direct mail test. Fortunately, Citizens For's 50,000-piece test was a big success. It yielded 800 members whose average contribution was $22.50. The group grossed only $18,000 from this initial effort but was encouraged to proceed because six of the ten lists tested were at break-even or better. Besides, one of two package variations substantially outperformed the other. The successful package variation and six of the ten lists accounted for the lion's share of the $18,000 in revenue, strongly suggesting that in a second, "continuation" or "rollout" mailing that eliminated poorly performing lists, response to the winning package will be much higher overall.

People Against

Following a contrasting strategy, People Against is also on the road to a successful long-term direct mail fundraising program. With an identical 1.6 percent response and $22.50 average gift, the well-funded group shrugged off its $7,000 loss and is ready to pull out the stops to launch a major nationwide campaign.

Because of their sharply different financial circumstances, Citizens For and People Against follow different strategies even though the results of their initial test mailings were statistically identical. Citizens For sets out to tap the profit potential of its direct mail fundraising program at the earliest possible opportunity, while well-heeled People Against has its sights set on a more distant future.

Neither strategy is "better" than the other. Each serves the group's strategic requirements.

Opposite is a schematic representation of the two groups' contrasting experiences, year by year, in the five-year period following their initial tests.

In English, here's what that means:

Year One

■ Citizens For conducts four 75,000-piece donor acquisition mailings, for a total of 300,000 prospect letters, building its list from 800 at the outset to 5,300 by year's end. The proceeds from quarterly donor renewal mailings, combined with modest profits from prospecting, yield a net profit of over $45,000.

■ People Against aggressively pursues a growth strategy, mailing one million donor acquisition packages in the first year. While the list grows to more than 12,000 by the end of this period, profits from an intensive donor renewal program aren't enough to erase the loss. People Against ends the first year another $7,000 in the red.

Year Two

■ Citizens For continues to pursue its cautious, cash-flow-conscious approach, mailing just 300,000 acquisition appeals (as it will each year throughout the five-year period). The donor list passes the 9,000-mark by year-end. Aggregate net profits for the full year top $81,000.

■ Having built an active donor list of over 12,000 names at a net cost of a little more than $1 per name, People Against calculates it's not being sufficiently aggressive. It steps up its prospecting effort to 1.5 million letters in the second year. Despite this increased investment, the program nets $217,000, because donor renewal efforts yield large profits.

Year Three

■ The Citizens For list passes the 12,500 mark and the organization tops $139,000 in net direct mail revenue after paying all program costs and fees.

■ People Against's file nears 50,000 names by year's end after another 2 million acquisition letters. Net profits for the year are $492,000.

Year Four

■ Citizens For's 300,000-piece prospecting program pushes the donor list to over 15,500. With stepped-up resolicitation efforts, net cash yield from the program is $177,000.

■ Dropping 2.5 million prospect letters, People Against's file tops 73,500. Net program revenue is $825,000 for the year.

Year Five

■ Citizens For has over 18,000 donors by the end of the year. Net profits for the year are $211,000.

■ People Against drops 3 million acquisition letters, and its file passes the 100,000 mark. Its net for the year is $1,200,000.

The Five-Year Period

■ Citizens For has mailed 1,550,000 donor acquisition letters and netted $648,000 from direct mail after paying all costs and fees. Its file includes 18,000 active donors.

■ People Against has dropped more than 10 million prospect letters and built an active donor list of 100,000 names. Its five-year net profit is $2,728,000.

In other words, People Against—with the resources and the grit to push the limits of the market in its donor acquisition program—has built a file that is *five times* as large and netted more than *four times* as much as Citizens For.

This doesn't mean that the more aggressive strategy is "better" than the other. I confess that the entrepreneur in me finds People Against a more interesting organization. Its "high risk—high gain" philosophy is the way to make the most of what direct mail has to offer. But such a hard-hitting approach may be inappropriate and even impossible for Citizens For, no matter what its inclinations might be.

However, the capital and the level of risk actually involved in even the larger of these two programs was quite small compared to the ultimate returns from the program.

■ Citizens For and People Against advanced $25,000 each for their test mailings. Citizens For needed no more than another $15,000 to launch its first 75,000-piece "continuation" or "rollout" mailing, and nothing more thereafter. Its total investment was $40,000. Measured

CITIZENS FOR				
	PROSPECT	LIST	RENEWAL	NET
	50,000	800		($7,000)
YEAR 1	300,000	5,300	$12,200	45,600
YEAR 2	300,000	9,164	36,160	81,320
YEAR 3	300,000	12,564	86,913	139,370
YEAR 4	300,000	15,557	112,484	177,726
YEAR 5	300,000	18,190	134,986	211,478
TOTAL	1,550,000	18,190	$382,743	$648,494

PEOPLE AGAINST			
PROSPECT	LIST	RENEWAL	NET
50,000	800		($7,000)
1,000,000	12,300	$39,300	(7,400)
1,500,000	28,800	164,400	217,800
2,000,000	49,800	314,400	492,800
2,500,000	73,550	493,400	825,800
3,000,000	100,550	696,400	1,206,800
10,050,000	100,550	$1,707,900	$2,728,800

Investment in direct mail can pay big dividends.

against a five-year net of nearly $650,000, that seems puny. It's a return on investment of *1,625 percent!* I don't know about your banker, but mine thinks that's not a bad deal for Citizens For!

- By contrast, though, People Against made out like a bandit. For its first 250,000-piece rollout, the group had to add about $40,000 to the $18,000 contributed in response to the initial test mailing. Its banker was a *little* worried, but from that point on, the program was self-sustaining. Profits from resolicitations funded the larger and more costly acquisition mailings in Years Three, Four, and Five—and left a *lot* to spare. A total cash investment of $65,000 yielded more than $2,700,000 in net revenue available to finance People Against's programs—a return on investment of *4,154 percent.*

Admittedly, that's one of the more advantageous ways to view the return on an investment in a direct mail fundraising program. A more conservative method is to examine the amount of capital tied up in the program at any one time—that is, the funds needed to pay the bills for those large, repeated donor acquisition mailings—and compare it with the net returns for that year only.

For Citizens For, the total financial exposure (or "investment") never exceeded $40,000—the approximate total cost of one of its 75,000-piece prospecting efforts plus one of its larger donor resolicitation mailings that might have been conducted at about the same time. In its first year, then, Citizens For's return on investment calculated in this manner was 113%. In Year Five, it was 528%.

For People Against, the capital required to finance continuing direct mail operations rose perceptibly as the scale of prospecting grew. In Years One and Two, People Against needed up to $130,000, and even in the second year net profits of $217,000 represented a return of only 167%. By Year Five, the group needed to devote nearly twice as much cash to cover ongoing program costs. Current capital investment of about $250,000 yielded net profits of over $1,200,000—a return of 480%.

Of course, there's another thing about bankers (as well as the trustees and executives of most charities): *they don't like risk.*

Without question, Citizens For's strategy entailed lower risks than that of People Against. While we tell our clients (and ourselves) that the risks are very limited in a carefully managed direct mail fundraising program, they're nonetheless real.

I've never yet lost a mailing because a mail truck caught fire—but such things have happened to others (on exceedingly *rare* occasions). And from time to time we've seen mailing results dip, sometimes very sharply, because of headline-grabbing catastrophes such as a stock market crash or a massive earthquake. It makes no sense to deny these problems—and even less to let them stop you from mailing.

The only way I know to address the problem of risk is to *manage* it, expecting occasional setbacks and maintaining the program's momentum in spite of them. As the leader of almost any successful new enterprise—whether a business or a nonprofit organization—will tell you, the only reliable way to achieve success is to keep plugging away, day after day, week after week. The rewards don't often come quickly. But, ultimately, the profits from a well-conceived and well-managed direct mail fundraising program may justify not just a little risk but a lot of hard work as well.

The approaches followed by Citizens For and People Against represent just two of many possible alternative strategies. Among others:

- Seeking huge numbers of donors at gift levels under $10 on the average and resoliciting them as frequently as every week. Programs of this type may entail tens of millions of prospect letters annually, and donor-files consisting of hundreds of thousands of names.
- Investing large sums in costly prospect packages in order to acquire new donors at a high entry level ($50 and up for single gifts, and $10 to $25 per month in "pledge" or "sustainer" programs), and investing more in "upgrading" them to even more generous levels of support.
- Establishing an arbitrarily low initial membership fee of $5 or $10 to build the largest possible membership with attractive (and expensive) benefits that cost you a lot more than the entry-level dues—and then identifying and upgrading those members willing and able to provide significant gifts.
- Acquiring "qualified" (proven) prospective donors at little or no cost through some form of sweepstakes offer, thus allowing more cost-efficient donor acquisition and building large lists that will generate substantial rental revenue.

While the possibilities aren't genuinely endless, they might as well be. After all, there are more than 96 million households in the United States, and there's probably somebody in the industry who thinks that just about every one of them is a good candidate for someone's direct mail fundraising program.

Are we having fun yet?

I'm sure it's becoming clear by now: if you've turned to direct mail as a way to grow, to diversify your sources of funding, and to broaden your financial base, you've gotten into a waiting game.

In the hypothetical cases of Citizens For and People Against as sketched out above, you can detect some of the trade-offs you're likely to confront—often a matter of *time versus money*. To cast a little more light on these issues, here are two concrete, real-life examples.

The Coalition

Two years and seven months have gone by—and *finally* The Coalition's direct mail fundraising program has gone into the black. We've mailed 800,000 prospect letters, yielding 12,400 new donors at a net cost of $49,000, or $3.95 per name. Donor resolicitation profits of $130,000 have barely covered this loss plus other costs and fees totaling $81,000. After raising a grand total of $557,000, The Coalition has netted the munificent sum of $1,500 through its direct mail fundraising program.

What could possibly make this program a good deal for The Coalition? Here are four of the reasons:

1. Major donor revenue— From the outset, The Coalition has been systematically approaching the most generous donors acquired in our direct mail program—treating them as *prospects* for larger gifts. In this aggressive effort, The Coalition's development department has netted more than $300,000 in just the first two years and seven months. They'll derive hundreds of thousands, perhaps eventually millions more, from these same donors in the years ahead.

2. Public relations value— The Coalition's message has already reached over a million people through direct mail, including a great many national opinion leaders. The Coalition's public profile has risen perceptibly in these first few years, in part due to the added exposure afforded by direct mail. As a public advocacy organization with a continuing need for publicity, this has great value for The Coalition—estimated to be worth $250,000 at the very least.

3. Future direct mail revenue— Starting virtually from scratch, we've already built an active donor list of 13,000 names. While profits from The Coalition's donor resolicitations were limited in the first two years, averaging about $6,000 per mailing, they've been running two or three times that much in the third year. (This is due in part to the greater economies of mailing to a larger list). In the next twelve months that list will *net* The Coalition more than $200,000 in direct mail revenue alone—*after* deducting all consulting and program management fees and the continuing costs of acquiring new donors at the rate of $4 to $6 per name.

4. List rental revenue— The Coalition may now choose to increase its current revenue by offering its list of 13,000 donors for rental to approved nonprofit mailers. If it pursues this option aggressively, it can net upwards of $25,000 per year for the next year or two.

In other words, even this seemingly lackluster program hasn't just broken even. The Coalition has directly received costly services, or cash from collateral fundraising, to the tune of more than $550,000. This includes $300,000 in net revenue from major donor fundraising and $250,000 in public relations value but doesn't count potential list rental revenue. The net result? *Doubling* the immediate returns from the program. Because of the contribution direct mail made to The Coalition's major donor fundraising program—properly seen as a long-term development effort—the real net value of the thirty-one-month campaign was probably nearer $1 million.

In this case, a $38,000 investment in an initial direct mail fundraising test accomplished exactly what it was supposed to do. Direct mail has planted a tree that will go on bearing fruit for The Coalition for many years to come.

The Institute

In six years, The Institute's direct mail fundraising program has netted $3.4 million from gross receipts of $6.5 million.

Beginning with just 200 donors, The Institute has acquired a total of more than 50,000 contributors. The average contribution of their resolicitation gifts was an unusually high $64.

A grand total of 4.6 million letters has yielded 114,000 contributions averaging $50—gross revenue of $5.7 million. Telephone fundraising and other collateral efforts produced another $800,000.

The Institute posted a net profit from direct mail operations of $119,000 in its very first year. In Year Two, net revenue topped $290,000. By Year Five—the high point of the program—the net approached $900,000.

The dramatic growth of The Institute's direct mail fundraising program paralleled the growth of its operating budget—from $300,000 in Year One to $2.5 million in Year Five. Many of the new funds raised in large gifts came from donors originally acquired through direct mail.

In this apparently idyllic picture, however, there are hidden massive problems. They're best highlighted by the fact that The Institute's net from direct mail dropped precipitously, from almost $900,000 in the fifth year to barely more than $500,000 in the sixth. The seventh year was worse. A *lot* worse.

How could such a thing happen, with a donor list of 50,000 names? It occurred for one simple reason:

The Institute decided to stop prospecting.

After a massive prospecting binge, The Institute virtually ended its donor acquisition efforts. Because response rates were dropping, and The Institute's management was preoccupied with internal management issues, the organization cut its prospecting volume from 1.7 million letters in the fifth year to fewer than 300,000 in the sixth.

This shortsighted decision curtailed The Institute's future growth. It also cut off the rich supply of fresh, responsive new donors that made it possible for the group to have netted almost a million dollars in a single year.

Some people speak of direct mail fundraising as a treadmill. If you're among the minority of nonprofit organizations able to get up to speed, you can climb on the belt—but getting off is a lot more difficult. The Institute's experience illustrates one aspect of this problem. The principal lesson its program illustrates is this:

You can't expect to build a list of loyal and responsive donors through direct mail and then simply leave the game.

Direct-mail acquired donors can't be expected to sustain a nonprofit's continuing operations at the same level indefinitely. People die or move without leaving forwarding addresses. Their financial circumstances change. So do their interests and loyalties. The cumulative effect of these factors is called "attrition." Because attrition literally decimates the typical donor-file each year, direct mail fundraising requires *continuous* prospecting.

Direct mail is a *process*, not a passing event.

There's no point where the process ends or achieves perfection. It's a continual search for new marketing concepts that serve your strategic needs because they work a little better than the old ones.

The way we develop those new concepts is through "testing."

Testing, testing, testing— until you're blue in the face

Every once in a rare while, we'll hit the nail on the head with a powerful marketing concept—a seemingly perfect marriage of package and lists—at the very beginning of a new program. Our "control" package—the standard-bearing donor acquisition appeal we keep mailing, over and over again—may emerge more or less wholly formed from a successful initial test. I've seen it happen more than once.

But, much more often, it takes two or three tries, and months or years of step-by-step refinements, to produce a workhorse prospecting package that will build a large, responsive donor-file. And then, sometimes quite suddenly, that package will "die," and you'll have to come up with another one very quickly.

A donor acquisition program might not hit its stride until the third or fourth year, or even later. This may be due to the organization's gradual accumulation of credibility and public recognition, to some shift in public sentiment about the issues it's addressing, or to changed attitudes in the organization's top management. But chances are it has a lot more to do with the cumulative value of thoughtful, systematic testing.

Now here's what I mean by a *"test"*:

■ You might, for example, want to know whether the response to your prospect package will rise significantly if you suggest a lower minimum gift in the letter and on the response device. Currently, the package urges a contribution of $25 or more. You want to lower the overall donor acquisition cost. So you decide to test whether suggesting a $15 minimum will lift the response rate sufficiently without forcing the average gift to drop in proportion.

- To determine this, you'd take two equal and statistically equivalent groups of names from the same pool of lists. You'd mail one group a package with the $25 "ask," the other with the $15 suggested minimum.

In theory, direct mail testing such as this will enable you to discover the perfect combination of offer, package, and postage—and ride off into the sunset, forever financially secure.

The reality's a little different. Well, a *lot* different.

For one thing, there are literally *innumerable* possible tests in a direct mail fundraising program. It's sometimes damnably difficult to figure out what's important to test and what isn't—particularly when your budget is strictly limited. Too much testing can eat up all the profits from your direct mail program.

In a program of modest scope, it's especially important to test only those elements that are "significant." A wholly new acquisition package built around a new marketing concept is likely to be a significant test. Most of the time, so are meaningful variations in the offer (or "ask"), in the copy that appears on the outer envelope (the "teaser"), or in the postage rate used. But any or all of these might be insignificant under some circumstances.

Another problem with the proposition that rigorous testing will show the way to optimal results is that it's often difficult to design tests that are statistically meaningful. In most situations, it requires many tens of thousands of names to establish confidence in the results of such things as price or postage testing. And even when you're able to test in these relatively large quantities, you'd be well advised to view the results with caution—no matter what the statisticians tell you.

Time and again, I've seen results vary twenty percent or more on even very large samples on which the variation was supposed to be no greater than five or ten percent. According to experts in statistics, variations this great shouldn't have occurred more often than one to five percent of the time. I suspect it *often* occurs, and so do some other direct mail fundraisers.

To test the validity of this proposition, on two occasions my colleagues and I arranged what we were assured were rigorous conditions. We split large groups of letters into two statistically identical groups to see the effect of random variation. There was *no* difference between the two groups in package, postage, list, or any other controllable factor. All we were testing was the extent to which two or more equal samples would produce equal results when simultaneously mailed identical packages.

On both occasions, random variation had a greater effect than statistical theory said it should. Others have had similar experiences.

Rather than chase down a technical explanation for these anomalies, however, I prefer to hold my clients' losses to a minimum and trust as little as possible in statistics—*except* when mailing quantities and testing budgets are big enough to add an extra margin of safety.

MINIMUM GIFT SUGGESTED	ACTUAL AVERAGE GIFT	RESPONSE RATE	COST PER DONOR ACQUIRED	NUMBER OF DONORS ACQUIRED IN 1 YEAR WITH $50,000 INVESTMENT
$15	$17	1.3%	$7	7,142
$25	$23	0.9%	$11	4,545

The amount you ask for can have extensive implications.

Why, then, when the results may not be statistically reliable, do we bother to test such things as offers, teasers, or postage? The answer is simple: *by and large, testing works.*

Testing works because we test with expectations, and we incorporate the results of our tests into future packages when our expectations are confirmed. Over time—sometimes even retesting vital elements two or three times—we're likely to learn valuable lessons that will enable us to upgrade a tolerably workable control package into one that's truly responsive.

Through testing—lifting response by ten percent with this little change and five percent with that one—we may eventually cut the donor acquisition cost by fifty or seventy-five percent. Testing may, and often does, bring new life into a prospecting program by permitting us to expand the volume and more quickly build large donor-files. In larger donor resolicitation programs, too, it can sometimes dramatically increase net revenue by helping establish the most cost-effective use of postage, packaging techniques, suggested contributions, and the like.

Testing is *not* limited to large direct mail programs. Almost any mailing of 10,000 names or more affords opportunities to test. Smaller quantities limit the options and make testing a long, drawn-out process. They demand extra care and greater patience. But the payoff can be just as dramatic in the end.

A "test" is just as real a mailing as one that's called something else. One person's small test is another's huge prospect mailing. They both have to be evaluated in terms of costs and benefits.

Be sure you don't fall prey to the common but costly mistake of evaluating test results only in terms of their actual costs. Testing is often expensive, because it may involve added creative, production, and even management costs—all of which need to be factored out when analyzing the outcome of a test. Otherwise, you'll be comparing expensive apples to cheap oranges. Testing costs should be considered part of the overhead of the direct mail fundraising program as a whole.

Now, it's not enough to design the tests. You've got to read and *use* the results—and that may be more easily said than done. They may conflict with the findings of earlier tests or with each other. With different goals in mind, interpretations may vary. And errors in the "letter-shop" (where mailings are addressed and assembled) may call the results into question.

But the biggest danger in testing is that equivocal results—or anxiety about poor results—might tempt you to delay future mailings.

Important as your test results might be, chances are, in a successful, ongoing direct mail fundraising program, you'll be better off mailing blind than waiting for a definitive reading. Your biggest mistake may be not to mail at all.

---

five

Getting the most from your donors

The four stages of a donor's life

MOST DONORS ACQUIRED BY DIRECT mail will support your organization in an active way for only a short time. A smaller number will remain with you for many years, completing the full cycle of donor life. That cycle has the following four stages:

1. Interest

Among those relatively few recipients of your donor acquisition package who spend more than the eight seconds it takes to decide to throw it away, you'll create some level of awareness about your organization and its work. A minority of those people will, in turn, demonstrate their interest by mailing you first-time gifts.

You can't count on these people as committed donors. They're simply declaring they've gotten a good first impression of you. Now you've got to convince them you're worthy of their support.

2. Support

Through the conversion process your donor re-solicitation program is designed to promote, you'll convince a majority of your one-time donors that your work warrants active support. The second, often more generous, gift you elicit from a new donor is a more meaningful statement of

conviction. She may well be a candidate now for a more substantial role in your organization.

3. Commitment

In response to your efforts to upgrade your donors, many will enter onto a level of financial commitment meaningful to you as well as to them. But to take this big step toward a major gift may require substantial personal contact as well as months or years of donor education through such means as newsletters and in-depth reports on your activities.

It's important, too, that you do everything possible to make the donor's experience rewarding for her as well as for you. Recognize her contribution in a public way, if she wishes, and thank her—not just with an impersonal note but warmly and often.

4. Legacy

A continuing process of cultivation, education, and appreciation will induce some of your major donors to regard their participation in the work of your organization as one of their major contributions in life. These are the people who will serve as volunteers—perhaps even on your board of trustees. They'll talk about your work among friends and family, make sizable annual gifts, establish planned giving programs, or remember

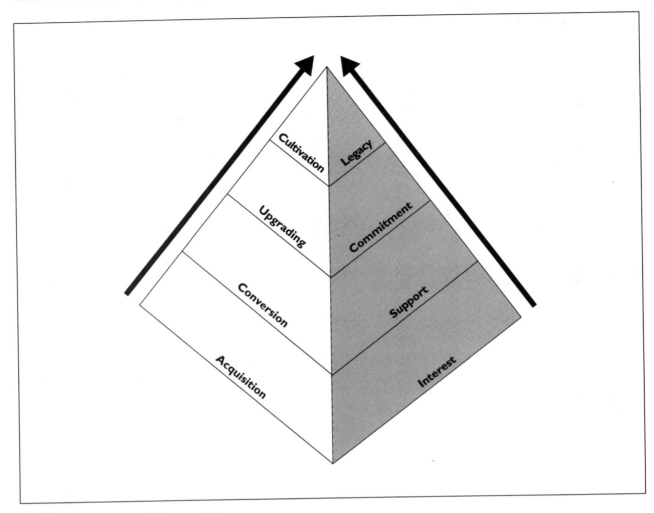

The four stages of donor life

you in their wills. Ultimately, the bequests and other major gifts you receive from these exceptionally strong supporters may dwarf the contributions from all your other donors combined. They're a living reminder that fundraising is a long, long process.

You'll derive the full value from your direct mail fundraising program only if your development staff is capable of working with your donors at every one of these four stages. Direct mail can start—even, in some cases, jump-start—the development process. But fundraising is a flesh-and-blood relationship that ultimately requires personal contact to realize its true potential. Far too many fundraisers regard direct mail-acquired donors as numbers. But they're people. People of true value.

What's a donor worth?

Sentimental considerations aside, it's entirely possible for an organization with at least a four-year track record in direct mail to calculate with meaningful precision the value it derives from the average new donor. It's rarely *easy* to do so. But there are at least three methods that can help you get a handle on this fundamental question.

Method One

By studying your donor renewal rates, you may be able to determine the average "life" of your donors. In a typical direct mail fundraising program, that averages out to about 2.6 years, or 31 months. During that time, the typical donor's two or three renewal gifts will average about twenty to twenty-five percent higher than her first gift. If she joined you with a contribution of $25, that means you'll likely receive another $90 (three times $30).

If the *average* gift in your acquisition program is as high as $25, this arithmetic is realistic. If the

*Assumes 25% shrinkage over previous year—and 15% increase in response rate and in average gift amount.
**Assumes 90% of members will receive renewal series.

	QUANTITY MAILED	COST PER 1000	RESPONSE RATE	CONTRI-BUTIONS	AVERAGE GIFT AMOUNT	GROSS REVENUE	*NET REVENUE
Year One							
Acquisition Mailing	100,000	$300	1.00%	1,000	$25	$25,000	($5,000)
Special Appeal 1	1,000	500	9.00%	90	43	3,870	3,370
Special Appeal 2	1,000	600	6.00%	60	36	2,160	1,560
Special Appeal 3	1,000	700	8.00%	80	38	3,040	2,340
Special Appeal 4	1,000	450	5.00%	50	34	1,700	1,250
Special Appeal 5	1,000	500	8.00%	80	38	3,040	2,540
Renewal 1**	950	500	19.00%	181	25	4,513	4,038
Renewal 2	770	500	16.00%	123	23	2,832	2,447
Renewal 3	646	500	11.00%	71	22	1,564	1,241
Renewal 4	575	500	9.00%	52	22	1,139	851
Renewal 5	524	500	6.00%	31	21	660	398
Renewal 6 (phone)	492	2,000	14.00%	69	35	2,411	1,427
Pledge Commitments	1,000	1,000	3.00%	30	240	7,200	6,200
TOTALS/YEAR ONE	**109,957**					**$59,128**	**$22,662**
Renewal Rate			**52.68%**				
Net Revenue Per New Member							**$22.66**
Year Two							
Special Appeal 1*	750	500	10.40%	78	49	3,857	3,482
Special Appeal 2	750	600	6.90%	52	41	2,142	1,692
Special Appeal 3	750	700	9.20%	69	44	3,015	2,490
Special Appeal 4	750	450	5.80%	44	39	1,701	1,363
Special Appeal 5	750	500	9.20%	69	44	3,015	2,640
Renewal 1*	750	500	21.90%	164	29	4,722	4,347
Renewal 2	586	500	18.40%	108	26	2,851	2,558
Renewal 3	478	500	12.70%	61	25	1,536	1,297
Renewal 4	417	500	10.40%	43	25	1,098	889
Renewal 5	374	500	6.90%	26	24	623	436
Renewal 6 (phone)	348	2,000	16.10%	56	40	2,256	1,559
Additional Pledges	750	1,000	2.00%	15	180	2,700	1,950
TOTALS/YEAR TWO						**$29,516**	**$24,705**
Renewal Rate			**61.06%**				
Net Revenue Per New Member							**$24.71**
Year Three							
Special Appeal 1*	563	500	12.00%	68	57	3,839	3,557
Special Appeal 2	563	600	7.90%	44	48	2,116	1,778
Special Appeal 3	563	700	10.60%	60	50	2,996	2,603
Special Appeal 4	563	450	6.70%	38	45	1,695	1,441
Special Appeal 5	563	500	10.60%	60	50	2,996	2,715
Renewal 1*	563	500	25.20%	142	33	4,687	4,405
Renewal 2	421	500	21.20%	89	30	2,713	2,503
Renewal 3	332	500	14.60%	48	29	1,408	1,243
Renewal 4	283	500	12.00%	34	29	989	847
Renewal 5	249	500	7.90%	20	28	547	422
Renewal 6 (phone)	229	2,000	18.50%	42	46	1,965	1,506
Additional Pledges	563	1,200	1.50%	8	170	1,434	759
TOTALS/YEAR THREE						**$27,385**	**$23,780**
Renewal Rate			**66.75%**				
Net Revenue Per New Member							**$23.78**
TOTAL/THREE YEARS						**$116,029**	**$71,147**
Net Revenue Per New Member Over 3 Years							**71.15**

There is a simple way to calculate long-term value.

average is much lower, it may not be true. Donors of less than $15 are less likely to renew.

After deducting applicable renewal costs and fees, your net from this source should be about

YEAR	ONE	TWO	THREE	FOUR
Number of members retained	1,000	600	420	328
Average gift including dues	$25.00	$27.50	$30.25	$33.28
Average number of gifts per member	1.3	1.3	1.3	1.3
Other income from same members	$1,000	$660	$462	$360
Number of monthly sustainers	20	44	57	63
Average annual income per sustainer	$163	$171	$180	$189
GROSS INCOME	$36,764	$29,650	$27,162	$26,462
Acquisition cost per member	$5.00			
Membership renewal cost per member	$.00	$1.95	$1.76	$1.58
Special appeal cost per member	$4.80	$5.28	$5.81	$6.39
Fundraising cost per sustainer	$8.40	$8.40	$8.40	$8.40
Other fundraising cost per member	$2.00	$2.20	$2.42	$2.66
TOTAL FUNDRAISING COST	$36,968	$6,028	$4,668	$4,013
NET INCOME	($204)	$23,622	$22,494	$22,450
COST PER DOLLAR RAISED	$1.01	$.20	$.17	$.15

There is a complicated way to calculate Lifetime Value.

$60. Add to that figure another $10 in net list rental revenue (five years at $2 per year), and the total value of that donor is $70. That's about $27 per year during the donor's "lifetime" of giving to your organization.

If you have a sophisticated development department, with an aggressive major donor program and other opportunities to elicit more frequent and larger-than-average gifts, that number may be twice as high, or even higher. Some well-established national charities, for example, expect to net an average of more than $70 *per year* from newly acquired members.

Method Two

By listing all the fundraising efforts you expect to undertake in the coming three years to elicit additional support from newly acquired donors or members, and by projecting the returns you might reasonably expect to receive, you can calculate the total expected revenue per donor. (It's easier if you do so for 1,000 or 10,000 donors and then divide accordingly, as in the table on page 65.)

Judging from the first method, it seems each new donor is worth a total of $70 to you. Using the second method, it's $71. Either way, an acquisition cost of $5 to $10 per name seems eminently reasonable. Two or three times that much, or even more, would make perfectly good sense if fast growth is essential to your strategy.

Setting that level, however, is a matter of tactics. The strategic problem is to determine how quickly you want your donor base to grow—and how much you can afford to invest in growth.

Method Three

This task becomes easier if you bring a truly long-term perspective to bear in your strategic planning. View direct mail fundraising over a *ten-year* period, and the picture will look genuinely rosy. Just take a look at the table above (which deals with a hypothetical organization different from the one depicted on the preceding

FIVE	SIX	SEVEN	EIGHT	NINE	TEN	TOTAL
278	242	218	198	181	164	
$36.60	$40.26	$44.29	$48.72	$53.59	$58.95	
1.3	1.3	1.3	1.3	1.3	1.3	13
$306	$266	$240	$218	$199	$181	$3,893
66	63	60	57	54	51	
$198	$208	$219	$230	$241	$253	
$26,636	$26,056	$25,902	$25,859	$25,782	$25,668	$275,942
$1.42	$1.28	$1.15	$1.04	$.93	$.84	
$7.03	$7.73	$8.50	$9.35	$10.29	$11.32	
$8.40	$8.40	$8.40	$8.40	$8.40	$8.40	
$2.93	$3.22	$3.54	$3.90	$4.29	$4.72	
$3,722	$3,492	$3,381	$3,313	$3,253	$3,200	$72,038
$22,914	$22,564	$22,521	$22,546	$22,529	$22,468	$203,904
$.14	$.13	$.13	$.13	$.13	$.12	$.26

page). In this third method of calculating the "Lifetime Value" of a donor or member, we take into account not only dues income but profits from special appeals, a lucrative monthly sustainer program, and other fundraising efforts, such as through merchandising, events, travel, or other products and services offered to members.

The upshot is that one thousand donors, acquired in Year One at an acquisition cost of $5 per donor, yield a total of $203,904 over ten years, or $204 per donor. That's net revenue averaging more than $20 per year for a decade. Doesn't $5 seem downright paltry by comparison?

However, the donor's "Lifetime Value" and the "donor acquisition cost" are statistical concepts. All your donors are *not* worth the same amount. Lifetime Value varies by the year in which a donor joins an organization, the list source, and the donor's giving characteristics.

Gift level may be the most significant of these variables. Of every 1,000 new donors you acquire through direct mail prospecting, fifty may give initial gifts of $50 or more, while one hundred each contribute less than $15. Those at the bottom of the scale may, in effect, be worth nothing at all to your organization, because testing repeatedly shows that donors of less than $15 are difficult to upgrade. By contrast, your new $50 donors may be worth a great deal indeed. They're by far the most likely of your new donors to remit additional gifts and are more likely to increase the level of their support.

There is a very high correlation between the level of the donor's original gift and the likelihood that donor will still actively support you more than a year later.

A rigorous Lifetime Value analysis of a fundraising program should break out the value of an organization's donors in categories determined by the size of their initial gifts. Among other things, an analysis of this sort might point the way toward a new approach to prospecting, emphasizing lists that yield above-average gifts.

■　■　■　■

Now let's get really technical for just a moment.

In any of these three methods, you should *reduce* the resulting Lifetime Value to its "net present value." This means taking into account one of two additional factors: either (a) the projected inflation rate, or (b) the return you might expect on a conservative investment if that's how you used your capital instead.

There are arguments for each of these choices, but I won't air them here. Except in times of rapid inflation, it's far more important to consider the issues that apply uniquely to direct mail fundraising. Of these issues, one of the most important is donor renewal.

Donor renewal concepts

If you're paying good money to recruit new donors, you'd better get your money's worth. That's what donor "renewal," or "resolicitation," is all about.

The fundamental principle of all professionally managed donor resolicitation programs is to *mail early and often*. Many people—especially, it seems, those who serve on nonprofit boards—find this maddeningly counterintuitive. Chances are you eat, sleep, and breathe your work. It may be difficult for you to understand that to someone who sent you a $25 check two or three months ago, your organization *might* not be the most important thing in her life this week. She may recall sending you a check, but the odds she'll remember what you told her in your acquisition letter are very slim.

Something important is lurking in the background here:

Direct mail fundraising is a form of advertising, which is based on *repetition*.

Unless you get back in touch with that new donor very quickly, and repeat the same themes and symbols in your resolicitation, she may no longer be a good prospect for additional support. Also, the chances are you'll have to ask her *several times* before you get a second gift.

You needn't take my word for this. Just try calling at random a few dozen of your new donors acquired by direct mail two or three months after you receive their first gifts (and before you mail them anything else). I predict you'll emerge the humbler from the experience.

It's conventional in the direct mail fundraising business to define everyone who's given you a single gift as a "donor." But in a real sense, a first-time contributor is really just a *qualified prospect*. She may be aware of your work, but she probably knows little about it, and she's clearly not a committed supporter. To tap the financial potential she represents, you'll have to educate and motivate her.

Psychologically, it's a big step for most people to send a *second* contribution. That implies a level of commitment many people are never willing to demonstrate. In fact, it's likely that anywhere from one-third to one-half of your first-time contributors will *never* give you a second gift. But once people have given *two* gifts, they're much more likely to contribute yet again, and perhaps much more generously.

In general, it's prudent to expect that no more than half your new donors will renew their support within the twelve-month period following their first gift. Of those who do so, a much larger proportion are likely to give again within the subsequent year. The progression is likely to look something like this:

	# years renewed	renewal rate
Year 1	new	50-60%
Year 2	1	60-70%
Year 3	2	68-78%
Year 4	3	75-85%
Year 5	4	80-87%
Year 6	5	83-90%
Year 7	6	85-91%
Year 8	7	87-91%
Year 9	8	88-91%
Year 10	9	89-91%

After 10 years of haphazard solicitation, 10 out of 100 donors remain. With 10% improvement in results each year, more than 30 remain.

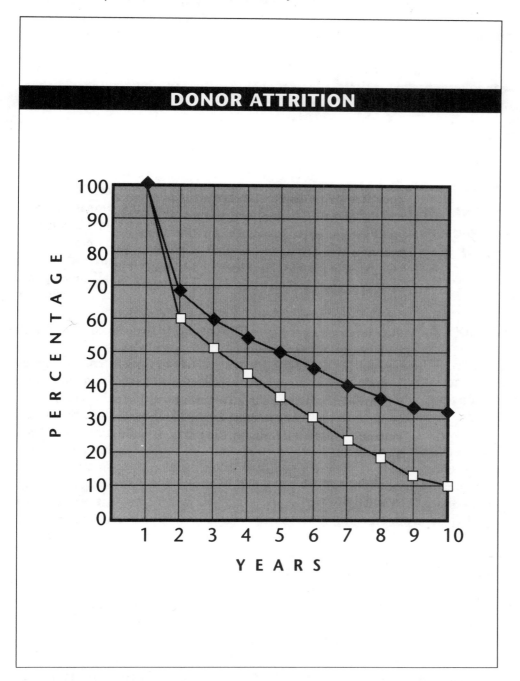

DONOR ATTRITION

With care and cultivation, you can retain many more donors.

The upper limit is imposed by death, illness, changing fortunes, shifting interests, and addresses lost when donors move.

In an organization that's been in operation for many years, it's common for more than sixty-five percent of *all* donors to renew their support in any given year.

The most urgent task of a donor renewal program is to convert the largest possible percentage of your recent first-time contributors into *donors*.

Increasing their renewal rate from forty percent to fifty percent, or from fifty to sixty, can have profound financial implications for your fundraising program in later years.

Just as you've invested in acquiring new donors, it's worth spending money to persuade them to become active supporters. This process, sometimes called "donor conversion," typically entails a quick thank-you in response to the first gift. Shortly afterwards, you begin mailing a series of donor resolicitation letters—once every two or three months for the next year or year-and-a-half.

A nearly equal priority in your donor renewal program is to *upgrade* your donors—to convince them to give bigger gifts.

Donor upgrading techniques favored by many nonprofit organizations include "gift clubs" and "monthly sustainer" programs. Both are devices to involve donors more intimately in the organization's work and to provide them with special rewards or recognition.

"Gift clubs" (also called "giving clubs" or "gift societies") provide a sense of belonging and special purpose to those donors who contribute large amounts of money. For example, you might offer "Life Membership" or special status within "The President's Circle" for $1,000 (paid in one sum or installments).

Giving clubs confer attractive privileges, benefits, and recognition not available to your other donors. Or you might choose to confer special status on those donors whose cumulative lifetime giving has exceeded that amount. A fully developed gift club can raise substantial sums from a large donor base, but it requires careful attention by staff. Many gift clubs are assigned full-time staff to deliver the promised benefits, privileges, and recognition and to attend to donors' correspondence and special requests.

"Monthly sustainer" or "pledge" programs offer new giving opportunities to small donors, whose gifts can add up very fast. At $10 per month, a donor's annual contribution is $120—far more than she's likely to give through dues notices and special appeals if her initial gift was a typical $15 or $20.

Thoughtfully designed and managed with skill and persistence, a sustainer program can attract as much as ten percent of your donors and become the financial backbone of your direct mail fundraising program. In one organization I'm familiar with, 4,500 of 45,000 donors contribute monthly gifts. In the aggregate, those monthly sustainers account for nearly one-third of the organization's $4.5 million operating budget. Like any successful gift club, however, a monthly pledge program requires patience, considerable staff time, and special attention.

Ultimately, however, your success in *cultivating* donors may have the greatest impact on your organization's long-term financial health. A handful of your direct mail donors may eventually become *major donors* whose individual gifts or bequests could possibly equal all the support you receive from the rest of your contributors combined.

Because your donors will become more and more valuable over time, your donor renewal program should seek to retain them as long as possible once you've converted them from one-time contributors into committed donors. "Donor retention" is a function of the impact and attractiveness of your programmatic work at least as much as it is of your fundraising efforts. But an effective donor renewal program can easily lift donor retention by ten percent or more each year. Over the long haul, that ten percent lift will have a profound impact on your budget. A ten percent annual improvement over typical donor renewal rates will *more than triple* the number of donors remaining active on your file after ten years! (See the graph on page 69.)

For many nonprofit organizations, a *membership* system makes good sense.

- Individuals recruited as members will expect you to ask for next year's dues.
- Because they've *chosen* to identify with your organization, they'll be actively interested in receiving news about your current activities, and they're good prospects for special appeals. One-third or more of your active members will send gifts over and above their dues.
- Members will feel more involved in your work and may more readily respond to invitations to become more active, perhaps as volunteers.

MONTH	DONOR ACQUISITION QUANTITY	DONOR RESOLICITATION QUANTITY	NEWSLETTER QUANTITY	TELEPHONE FUNDRAISING QUANTITY	TOTAL
Year 1					
Jan	50,000				50,000
Feb			500		500
Mar		500			500
Apr			500		500
May	100,000				100,000
Jun		1,000			1,000
Jul			1,500		1,500
Aug					
Sep	150,000	1,500			151,500
Oct			2,000		2,000
Nov					
Dec		3,000			3,000
Year 2					
Jan	150,000		2,500		152,500
Feb		4,000			4,000
Mar					
Apr		4,500	3,500		8,000
May	100,000				100,000
Jun		5,000			5,000
Jul			4,000	3,000	7,000
Aug		5,500			5,500
Sep	150,000				150,000
Oct		6,000	5,000		11,000
Nov					
Dec		7,000		2,000	9,000
Year 3					
Jan	250,000		5,000		255,000
Feb		8,000			8,000
Mar				4,000	4,000
Apr		9,000	7,000		16,000
May	100,000			3,000	103,000
Jun		9,000			9,000
Jul			7,500		7,500
Aug		9,000			9,000
Sep	200,000				200,000
Oct		10,000	8,000		18,000
Nov				6,000	6,000
Dec		11,000			11,000
TOTAL	**1,250,000**	**94,000**	**47,000**	**18,000**	**1,409,000**

Managing a long-term program is complex and demanding.

But members will expect you to deliver on your promises.

If your membership acquisition letter says members receive a quarterly newsletter, you'd better be sure you send one every three months.

If you've promised a "premium" for gifts above a certain level, you're in trouble if you don't have a system in place to send it out quickly.

Membership programs have many advantages, but they demand discipline and efficiency that carry price tags of their own.

Grassroots organizations often use "emergency" appeals to boost their fundraising revenue. Threatening to close the doors if there's poor response to an emergency letter may be an effective short-term fundraising technique, but it's unlikely to work as well the second time around. More important, it's shortsighted to "cry wolf."

Few donors will invest sizable sums in an organization that's on the brink of bankruptcy. A nonprofit group's long-term self-interest lies in enhancing, not undermining, the public's confidence in its integrity and stability.

Naturally, some emergency appeals reflect true emergencies: an earthquake or flood, an epidemic, the sudden cancellation of a major foundation grant. For the American Red Cross, for example, disaster appeals are a stock in trade. Donors *expect* to hear from them in time of emergency.

As with everything else in your direct mail fundraising program, your approach to donor renewal must relate to your organization's strategy.

■ For example, if your organization has a strong development department with a well-established fundraising program that includes major donor gift clubs, planned giving, bequests, and other special donor opportunities, your direct mail donor renewal program should probably emphasize donor education and *cultivation*. By using such tactics as highly personalized thank-you packages, thank-you phone calls, donor newsletters, and "High-Dollar" direct mail packages designed to elicit much larger gifts, your direct mail donor renewal program may prove to be a rich source of prospects for major gifts. The large contributions that ultimately result will represent a handsome return on a relatively modest investment in donor cultivation.

■ By contrast, if your organization has had neither the time nor the opportunity to build a strong overall development effort, your direct mail program may constitute a large share of your "major donor" fundraising efforts. If this is the case, your direct mail program needs to be as profitable as possible while also providing sufficient opportunities for donor *upgrading*, so you can get the most from your donors. This may mean mailing very selectively to your donors and treating the most generous of them to particularly strong, personalized packages and friendly phone calls. In effect, this approach mimics the personal attention major donors would get from a professionally run development department.

Sticking to the schedule

While you need to plan the frequency of your renewal mailings in the context of your organizational strategy, the rule of thumb we follow is to mail *more* often rather than less. In all likelihood, your net profits from direct mail will rise as you increase the frequency of appeals to your donors.

A friend once conducted a systematic, year-long test of this proposition. He divided a large, statistically homogeneous segment of his file into two equal groups, mailing one group only four special appeals that year and the other group eight. As might be expected, those donors who received eight letters didn't respond in such great numbers to each *individual appeal* as those who received only four. But the *net* returns from the group that received eight appeals were more than thirty percent higher. (See opposite page.)

Sticking to the schedule is the key to making a donor renewal system work consistently well. If your mailing schedule calls for eight donor resolicitations this year—roughly six weeks apart from one another—a slippage of ten days to two weeks for each of the first three mailings will mean you're likely to mail seven times, not eight. Another month's delay could cut your program down to six renewals. In that case, you won't be getting full value from your donors. The financial impact can be sizable. (See table on page 74.)

An intelligent donor renewal system is easily undermined by undue attention to our old nemesis, the fundraising ratio (the cost of a dollar raised). Let's say your board's fundraising chair tells you it's unacceptable to continue paying $0.38 to raise every dollar in your direct mail donor resolicitation program. She says you have to drive the ratio below $0.30.

That may be easy to accomplish, as you can see in the table on page 74. Here's how:

■ Reduce the frequency of your resolicitations (which will improve the response rate on each mailing).

■ Stop mailing to less recent and less generous donors (which will raise both the average gift and the response rate).

■ Mail cheaper packages (which might lower the average gift and the response rate but is also likely to raise proportionally more money for every dollar expended).

In this hypothetical resolicitation program, net profit from eight mailings is more than double the net profit from one mailing. And far more donors will remain active next year because they renew their support this year.

NUMBER OF RESOLICITATION MAILINGS PER YEAR	AVERAGE RESULTS FOR EACH MAILING INDIVIDUALLY		TOTAL NET ANNUAL PROFIT
8	Quantity mailed Percent response Average gift Cost per 1,000 Net revenue	30,000 7.5% $30 $750 $45,000	$360,000
7	Quantity mailed Percent response Average gift Cost per 1,000 Net revenue	30,000 8.0% $30 $750 $49,500	$346,500
6	Quantity mailed Percent response Average gift Cost per 1,000 Net revenue	30,000 8.5% $30 $750 $54,000	$324,000
5	Quantity mailed Percent response Average gift Cost per 1,000 Net revenue	30,000 9.0% $30 $750 $58,500	$292,500
4	Quantity mailed Percent response Average gift Cost per 1,000 Net revenue	30,000 10.0% $30 $750 $67,500	$270,000
3	Quantity mailed Percent response Average gift Cost per 1,000 Net revenue	30,000 12.0% $30 $750 $85,000	$256,500
2	Quantity mailed Percent response Average gift Cost per 1,000 Net revenue	30,000 15.0% $30 $750 $112,500	$225,000
1	Quantity mailed Percent response Average gift Cost per 1,000 Net revenue	30,000 20.0% $30 $750 $157,500	$157,500

One added resolicitation mailing can make a big difference.

In the example illustrated here, this combination of choices will succeed in raising the response rate from six percent to eight percent and the average gift from $35 to $40. The cost of the direct mail donor resolicitation program accordingly will drop from $128,000 to just $50,000.

The fundraising ratio thus will plunge from thirty-eight percent to twenty-six percent, an improvement that will please your fundraising chair—until you explain the disadvantages. Your net revenue will drop by $66,000, or nearly thirty-two percent, and your donor list will shrink by several thousand individuals. By mailing 100,000 fewer resolicitation letters, you won't just be cutting costs. You'll also be missing opportunities to convert new donors into active supporters and to persuade lapsed donors to return to the fold. Your organization would continue paying the price of this shortsightedness for years to come.

Many fundraisers resist this logic. Some have argued that donors to institutions such as universities, hospitals, or museums *expect* to receive fewer appeals than do supporters of, say, advocacy groups and medical research organizations. For example, the annual fund manager at a college may insist that her alumni will only give once per year. They'll complain if she asks more than once. To her I say, "Good luck!" A single appeal per year will *not* do the job.

Whether alumni, former patients, or arts patrons, *some* of your donors will ignore or mislay your one-time appeal, no matter how deeply committed they are. And *some* will feel neglected if you write them only once every year.

Remember: your donors are your friends. They *want* to hear from you.

Taking good care of your donors

At first, nearly all the donors you acquire from direct mail acquisition will be, for all intents and purposes, of equal importance. Initially, you'll have just a few thousand on file. Your biggest challenge then will be to find cost-effective ways to stay in touch with them and build their under-

	CURRENT RESOLICITATION SCHEDULE	REVISED RESOLICITION SCHEDULE	DIFFERENCE
Number of resolicitations	8	4	4
Average number of donors resolicited per mailing	20,000	15,000	5,000
Year's total resolicitation quantity	160,000	60,000	100,000
Number of gifts received	9,600	4,800	4,800
Average percent response per resolicitation mailing	6%	8%	33%
Year's total gross resolicitation revenue	$336,000	$192,000	$144,000
Year's total cost of resolicitation mailings	$128,000	$ 50,000	$ 78,000
Net resolicitation revenue	$208,000	$142,000	$ 66,000
Cost per dollar raised	$0.38	$0.26	32%

Cutting costs can be a losing proposition.

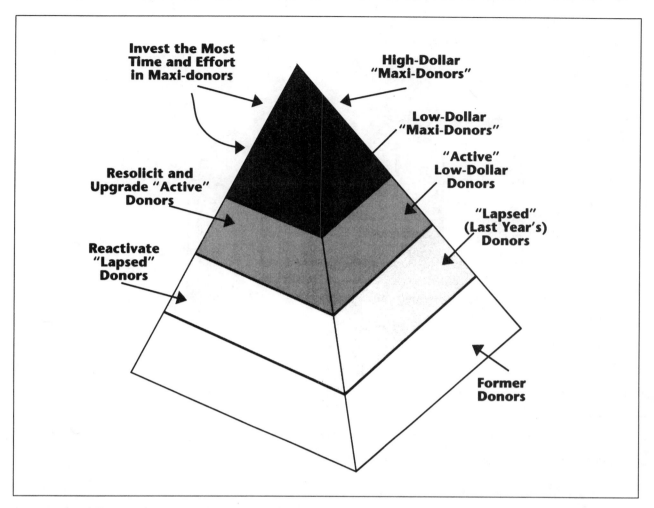

Invest the Most Time and Effort in Maxi-donors

High-Dollar "Maxi-Donors"

Low-Dollar "Maxi-Donors"

"Active" Low-Dollar Donors

Resolicit and Upgrade "Active" Donors

"Lapsed" (Last Year's) Donors

Reactivate "Lapsed" Donors

Former Donors

Some donors are more equal than others.

standing of your work. If you're lucky, you'll net at least modest amounts, which will help subsidize your prospecting program.

Once you're beyond the four- to six-thousand donor level, you can begin "segmenting" your file. "Segmentation" is the key to a profitable donor renewal program over the long term.

Segmentation is based on one simple truth: *some people give more money than others.*

In direct mail fundraising, segmentation—the division of your donor list into subgroups or "segments"—is usually based on three fundamental distinguishing characteristics:

- *Recency*—the date on which you received a donor's most recent contribution
- *Frequency*—how many gifts you've received from that donor either cumulatively or within the current calendar year, or how many years the donor has actively supported you

- *Gift amount*—generally stated as the highest previous contribution, but often inconveniently (and less usefully) presented as cumulative total giving or year-to-date total

However, the source of the donor's name and information may be of equal significance. For example, you can expect direct mail-acquired donors to be much more responsive to appeals sent by mail than are donors acquired through special events or telemarketing.

The fundamental principle of segmentation is this:

Those who've contributed most generously, most frequently, and most recently are your best prospects for additional gifts.

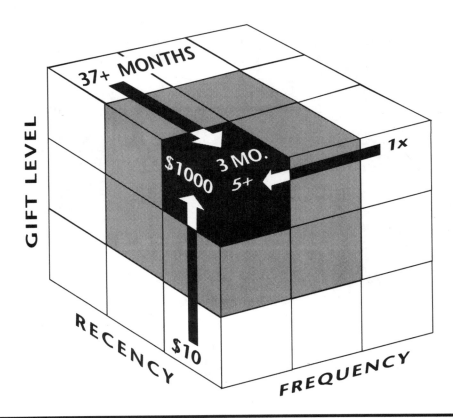

Recency, frequency, and gift level define donor segments.

These are the people to whom you should be paying the most attention and in whom you should be investing the most in your donor renewal efforts. We call them "Core Donors" or "Maxi-Donors." Depending upon the precise definition, they may include anywhere from fifteen to thirty percent of your file—but the chances are they contribute three-quarters or more of the net income from your fundraising program.

You may be tempted to refrain from resoliciting anyone who's just given you a gift, or even to methodically eliminate from later appeals those who respond to the first or second letter you've sent this year. In most cases, this is a very big mistake, for three reasons:

1. The special appeals you write are (or should be) one of your donors' primary sources of information about your work. Not to inform the donors who have shown the *most* interest in your organization reflects misguided priorities. Resolicitation is part of the process of "bonding" and cultivating your donors, some of them potential major contributors.

2. Your donors contribute to you from their *current* income. Most write checks that are small by their own standards, and many are willing to do so several times a year. By failing to solicit them regularly, you'll lose a great deal of money.

3. Recent contributors are *most* likely to give again. They're the most interested, the most responsive, and the best prospects for special opportunities such as monthly sustainer programs or gift clubs.

An intelligent approach to segmentation requires that you establish the most cost-effective frequency of contact with each segment of your donor file. You might choose to group the individuals on your list into four broad categories:

- *"Core Donors"* or "Maxi-Donors," including your most generous, most frequent and most recent contributors
- *"Active Donors,"* who aren't quite so generous, frequent, or recent as Maxi-Donors
- *"Lapsed Donors,"* whose last gift arrived at least a year or eighteen months ago but not longer than two or three years ago

- *"Former Donors,"* who haven't contributed for two or three years or more

It's unwise to treat all four of these groups in the same way.

The only segment that's really worth your full attention at all times are your *Core Donors*. You should be in touch with them no less frequently than once every two months (six times per year) and perhaps more often than once per month.

Active Donors may not respond well to such frequent contact. Four to six times per year should suffice.

You may recapture a significant proportion of *Lapsed Donors* with two, three, or four mailings this year.

The more recent of your *Former Donors* may be worth one or two last direct mail efforts this year—but probably not more.

The biggest cliché in fundraising is the "80-20 Rule": twenty percent of your donors will contribute eighty percent of your fundraising revenue, even though they may require only twenty percent of your fundraising budget. The other eighty percent, soaking up four-fifths of the budget, will yield only twenty percent of your revenue.

Identifying and cultivating your Core Donors—and treating other significant segments of your donor file in different but appropriate ways—is an effort to turn the "80-20 Rule" on its head.

Through segmentation, you can invest greater resources to maximize the returns from your most productive segments—and minimize the cost of working with those that are less productive. This will help ensure that you get the highest possible net profit from your direct mail fundraising program.

In the long run, however, your direct mail program may pay off even more handsomely with *major* gifts from a few individuals. As your donor list grows, you should put into place a system of "donor research" to determine whether new donors are good prospects for large gifts. These are the individuals you'll want to cultivate carefully. You'll write and call them personally and arrange face-to-face visits, if possible. Their contributions—amounting to many thousands of dollars—may represent the *real* payoff for all the hard work that's gone into your direct mail fundraising program.

You may wish to conduct donor research in-house, checking the local library's *Who's Who,* the *Foundation Directory,* Standard & Poor's *Register of Corporations, Directors and Executives,* and other likely sources of information about wealthy individuals.

Some large nonprofit institutions, especially colleges and universities, support substantial do-

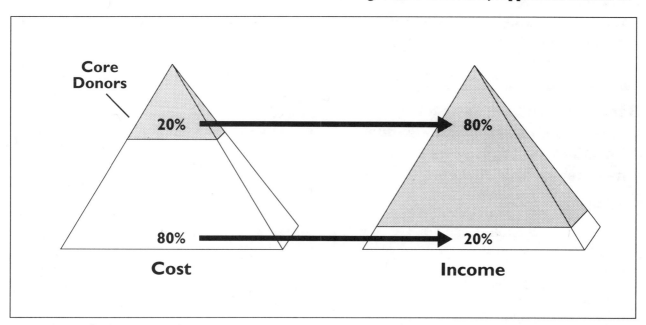

The 80-20 Rule: spending more on some donors will pay off.

nor research departments. If you have little or no development staff, you may conclude it's worth paying someone else to do the job of donor research. A variety of professional services are available in this important field. For example, CDA/Investnet (Ft. Lauderdale, Florida) compiles detailed reports on the investment holdings of major gift prospects on the basis of publicly available information. Grenzebach, Glier, & Associates, Inc. (Chicago, Illinois) and Marts & Lundy, Inc. (Lyndhurst, New Jersey) use computers (in different ways) to identify the best major gift prospects on an organization's donor file. The directories of vendors published by fundraising trade periodicals contain the names of other firms that provide similar services.

"Back-end" services

As your donor base grows, you'll probably begin paying more and more attention to two of the most nettlesome questions about direct mail fundraising:

- Who's going to count the money?
- And how are you going to keep track of all the people who give it to you?

It's a good idea to think through your answers to these questions *before* you mail your initial test. The decisions you make in this area of so-called "back-end" services are fateful—and they may not be obvious.

Here's the fundamental principle on which an intelligent back-end system for direct mail fundraising is based:

Donors are people, and they deserve to be treated as individuals. They also tend to give more money when they're treated well.

In practice, this means you'll need:

- A quick-turnaround donor acknowledgment program
- An extensive database maintenance system that includes almost every scrap of useful information your fundraising results can provide about each individual donor

- A meticulous system of data entry with built-in quality control procedures to maintain a file of the highest possible accuracy
- A working system for your staff to respond to individual donor questions and complaints in a timely and polite manner

The capacity to deliver all these services may cost you $2 to $3 per donor per year. Admittedly, such a costly back-end system may not work well for a direct mail fundraising program involving hundreds of thousands of $5 or $10 donors. Three dollars per year per donor will probably eat up too much of the profits. But a program in which the average gift is $15 or higher—thus allowing for upgrading—may not live up to its potential *without* such a labor-intensive back-end system. Careful list maintenance is necessary to ensure that you can send credible, personalized appeals.

About every six months, almost like clockwork, one of our longstanding clients used to ask me, "How big a computer do I need to hold my list? How much will a computer like that cost?" The question may appear disingenuous. Obviously, there's more involved than computer hardware. But it highlights one of the enduring sources of confusion in direct mail fundraising: whether to hire additional staff or train volunteers to provide back-end services instead of retaining a service bureau.

The best answer to that question (like most other things about direct mail) has its roots in your organizational strategy. With a multimillion-dollar direct mail fundraising program involving many tens or hundreds of thousands of donors in an intensive program of communications and resolicitation, an in-house service bureau might make sense. It might also be cost-effective at the other end of the scale, with a small, inactive direct mail program—if your staff or an exceptionally well-trained, disciplined, *long-term* volunteer can handle the job in a timely and consistent manner.

But most of the time, for direct mail fundraising programs of the type and the scale described in this book, keeping the work in-house makes no sense at all. An in-house system for back-end processing will burden your organization with specialized staff and computer hardware and software, and it will subject you to all the headaches entailed by running what is, after all, a business. Very few nonprofits can run such a business in a consistently efficient and cost-effective manner.

Once again, it's worth taking a leaf from the annals of the business world and asking yourself the single most critical question you can pose about your organization: *What business are you in?* With an aggressive direct mail fundraising program and a growing donor file to match, you could easily discover that you're really in the data processing business if you try to build an in-house service bureau—no matter what your mission statement might say. Willy-nilly, the tail wags the dog.

To avoid this problem, some organizations find it worthwhile to pay professionals to do the job *even if* they're convinced they can do it just as well and perhaps even more cheaply.

Back-end services require a respect for complex procedures and a compulsive attention to detail. The job looks deceptively easy—but it may require an investment of tens or hundreds of thousands of dollars in systems analysis, programming, training, and maintenance. The cost of the hardware is a minor consideration by comparison.

One alternative favored by many nonprofits is to buy or lease a specialized fundraising software program. There are many on the market, some offered in conjunction with dedicated hardware systems, others sold "in the can," with or without continuing technical assistance. If it works—and I've never actually talked to a totally satisfied customer—a system of this sort might lower your investment in an in-house service bureau. But it begs the question of where the job should be done. I believe that, in most circumstances, the wisest course is to retain a specialized service bureau to manage all your back-end operations and be held accountable for doing the job right.

There are at least four separate (though not necessarily separable) tasks in a back-end system:

- *"Cashiering"*—processing and depositing contributions to your bank account.
- *"Caging"*—processing and recording the list-by-list and package-by-package information encoded on the response devices in your mailing and outputting it in the form of "flash-counts." (Flashcounts are progress reports on your mailing that break down the results by list or segment.)
- *"Donor acknowledgment"*—thanking your donors, and perhaps asking for another gift at the same time.
- *"List maintenance"*—updating your donor file, recording both new information and corrections to the old, and providing periodic analytical reports that depict the cumulative impact of all your fundraising programs, segment by segment.

In the earliest stages of your direct mail fundraising program, it may be most efficient for your staff to tend to cashiering, caging, and donor acknowledgments. If you have an effective list maintenance system in place, it might also be worthwhile to fold in the early test results. But once your direct mail program is under way, it makes sense to transfer your list maintenance to professionals. Ideally, you'll find a service bureau that caters to direct mail fundraisers and offers an integrated system of caging, list maintenance, and donor acknowledgments.

You might find it advantageous to continue cashiering your direct mail returns in-house, especially if they're just one of several active sources of income and you're already equipped to process large numbers of checks. In such circumstances, however, you'll need to transfer the raw data from your direct mail program to the service bureau on a timely basis.

As your direct mail fundraising program grows in scope and complexity, the demands on your back-end systems will increase geometrically. And just wait until you're ready to start using telephone fundraising, too!

The many uses of the telephone

Now, let me guess: you don't *like* the idea of telephone fundraising.

Chances are, you've got four or five objections to using what most people in the phone-calling business so clumsily refer to as "telemarketing":

- Phoning your donors seems intrusive.
- It's a technique widely known to be used by fraudulent charities.
- Telemarketing puts your organization's reputation at risk because you may not be able to exert direct control over the individuals who make the phone calls.

■ And, besides, you just hate it when somebody calls *you* at dinnertime to ask for money—and so does everyone you know!

Then why do so many organizations use the telephone so extensively in their fundraising programs?

The answer I give to that question is precisely the same as my response to those who ask why so many nonprofit groups use direct mail:

It works!

Now, please don't confuse telephone fundraisers with bucketshops peddling tickets by phone to charitable events. These high-pressure operations—most of them local, and some of them fly-by-night ventures that skip from one city to the next—are responsible for the lion's share of the public's complaints about telephone fundraising. They're also responsible for most of the fraud. Doubtless, some are honest, hardworking, and sincere. But many such operators exploit their employees, their clients (if in fact they're legitimate), and the public.

To me, telephone fundraising means using the telephone as a communications tool to connect a nonprofit with its supporters, almost always previous donors.

It's impossible to estimate with any accuracy how much money legitimate nonprofit groups raise by telephone in a year, but I'm certain the figure runs to many billions of dollars. So explosive has been the growth of telephone fundraising in recent years that what was a mere handful of firms offering these services at the beginning of the 1980s has become a large industry involving many hundreds of companies. And countless charities and public interest groups have established in-house phone banks operated either by volunteers or by professional staff.

Whenever you contact thousands of people—whether by telephone or by mail—some of them are bound to become irritated. There's no more effective or efficient method of communicating with members and supporters than by telephone—and no more efficient way to annoy at least a few of them.

Without telephone fundraising, however, many groups would raise substantially less money to support their programs. Most nonprofit organizations conclude, with varying degrees of regret, that they simply can't avoid using the telephone. Measured on a revenue-to-cost basis, or in terms of sheer net profits, there's often no way to beat it.

Yes, there are complaints. And, yes, individual donors *matter*.

We've found it's cost-effective to exert the utmost effort to mollify those few individuals—fewer than one percent—who become angry when we call them.

But it's a mistake to dwell upon donors' complaints. Many people—especially those who don't reside on either coast—actually *enjoy* the telephone calls we make on behalf of our clients.

Typically, the number of those who thank you for calling far exceeds the number who complain. Many people appreciate getting long-distance calls from groups they support. Each call is an opportunity to pass along a great deal of useful information to your members or donors, often correcting mistaken impressions or reminding them of past successes.

Whether conducted by a specialized telephone fundraising company, a commercial telemarketing service bureau, or an in-house phone bank, telephone fundraising has six principal applications in public interest fundraising:

1. Reactivating lapsed members— After you've reached the end of your rope through direct mail, and one more renewal notice simply isn't cost-effective, your best shot at recapturing lapsed members or donors is by phone. Normally, this is a break-even proposition, but only in a short-term perspective. After all, now you know how much your donors are worth! Some groups find they're worth enough—and telephone reactivation is effective enough—that it pays for them to call early in the renewal cycle, as the second or third effort in a series. (Keep in mind, though, that donors who are "recaptured" by telephone tend to be more responsive to future telephone appeals than to mail.)

2. Special appeals— To vary the rhythm and the medium of your contact with your donors, you'll probably find it profitable to conduct one or two special appeals each year by telephone. (Contact more frequently than every six months

Thank you, Jamie Q Sample, for your gift of $25.
Please send this notice and your check payable to
Wisconsin Public Television, at your earliest convenience.
We greatly appreciate your support.

YES! Here's my countdown gift to Wisconsin Public Television helping
WPT continue its tradition of educating and enlightening all the people
of our state. 521-0208-T1-Y-95178   05/16/94 TB55

Jamie Q Sample
123 Maple Street
Anytown, WI 00000

Please make your check payable to Wisconsin Public Television and return with this slip in
the envelope provided.

countdown

WISCONSIN PUBLIC TELEVISION

821 UNIVERSITY AVENUE
MADISON, WI 53706-1412

Pledge cards remind donors they promised to help.

may be ineffective or even counterproductive.) But if your donors pledge to contribute, it's important to follow through with several reminders to hold them to their word. Don't let them easily off the hook with direct mail appeals, which may request a lot less money than they've promised on the phone.

3. Upgrading donors— Through such means as specially named "gift clubs" and monthly pledge or sustainer programs, you can use telephone fundraising to increase the level of your donors' support for you. The phone allows a caller—a representative of your organization—to negotiate with the donor for a *specific* level of support. The caller can even negotiate convenient payment terms.

4. Donor acknowledgments— It may well be worth your while to call at least the more generous of your donors to thank them for their support. A thoughtful gesture of this sort may increase donor loyalty over the long term. For many groups, gifts of $100 or more are big enough to justify this type of red-carpet treatment.

5. Mail-phone appeals— Especially for your most generous donors, the considerable expense of combining one or more direct mail contacts with at least one telephone call—all for a single appeal—may pay off in a very big way if it's wisely planned and well executed.

6. Prospecting for new donors— Some nonprofit groups use the telephone to acquire new donors. In some circumstances, this may make a lot of sense. If your issue or project is hot enough, and available lists are strong enough, telephone acquisition will produce a high rate of response and possibly even yield net revenue for your organization. Especially if you combine telephone acquisition with aggressive donor resolicitation efforts, your overall cost of fundraising may be entirely reasonable.

Most of the time, however, telephone prospecting is a poor idea. It's often a more expensive mode of prospecting than direct mail. It's far more intrusive than calling your own donors, who are much more likely to want to hear from you. It may risk conflict with state charitable fundraising regulators. And, generally speaking, phone-acquired donors can only be resolicited cost-effectively by telephone.

In nearly every type of professionally executed telephone fundraising campaign, donors are asked to commit themselves to contribute a specific amount of money. That amount is then cited on a follow-up mailing, sometimes called a "pledge card" or "pledge reminder," and mailed as quickly as possible after the phone call, ideally within 24 hours. Some firms mail slightly different versions of their pledge cards to donors who indicate support but won't commit themselves to specific amounts.

While your specific objectives will surely vary from one type of telephone fundraising program to another, all six types have several advantages in common:

- *Net revenue*—This may be deferred revenue in the case of reactivation or prospecting efforts, but it's almost always the principal reason to employ telephone fundraising techniques.

- *Donor education*—By conveying a brief and clearly focused message in a comprehensive telephone "script," your donors are much more likely to *remember* you than if you mail an appeal to them, because the telephone is a "warmer," more intimate form of communication.

- *Two-way communications*—Unlike all but the rarest direct mail appeal, a telephone program gives your donors a chance to talk back and to feel more involved in your work.

- *Donor loyalty*—This may ultimately be the greatest advantage of telephone fundraising. Studies show that donors who are contacted by phone tend to remain donors longer and give more generously and more frequently than those who are contacted by mail alone.

Some organizations run telephone fundraising programs independently of their other development work. This is usually unwise. Telephone fundraising efforts are typically—and appropriately—conducted in conjunction with the overall direct mail program. The telephone is best seen as one more implement in the fundraiser's toolbox.

Think strategically. *Integrate* your direct mail and telephone fundraising efforts—even if you find, as some groups do, that their telemarketing efforts contribute as much as half of the net profits from the combined "direct response fundraising" program.

The mails and the telephone are merely different ways to communicate a common vision and sense of purpose to your donors.

For most members of a large national organization, the only *personal* contact available is by telephone. Intelligently managed telephone fundraising can add a warm, personal dimension to the relationship between you and your members, reinforcing your donor communications and fundraising programs (including direct mail) and building individual interest and loyalty.

Nothing else but face-to-face contact can match telephone fundraising as a way to *intensify* your organization's relationship with its members. The telephone is one of very few tools widely available to nonprofits that makes *person-to-person fundraising* possible.

However, telephone fundraising is fundamentally a financial proposition. The strongest case for it is that it makes money, and it usually does so in a way that's readily predictable. The numbers tell the most important part of the story.

What to expect from a telephone appeal

Assume your organization has 30,000 "current" donors on file. (These are contributors who, in this case, have sent you at least one gift within the past twelve months.) You've contracted with a professional telephone fundraising firm to conduct a special appeal designed to maximize net revenue and upgrade as many of your donors as possible. Here's what the numbers might look like:

- Of your 30,000 donors, the telephone fundraising firm you've hired feels that only 20,000 qualify as good prospects for telephone contact. The rest haven't given large enough gifts at any one time.

- A service bureau retained by the telephone fundraising firm will run a computer match against your remaining 20,000 donors to find their telephone numbers. With a little luck, they'll find sixty percent, or 12,000.

- Working on the basis of a script that you and the firm should devise together, paid callers will use WATS lines to contact those 12,000 donors, generally between the hours of 5:30 and 9:30 pm. Depending on how persistently they're told to keep trying if they get a busy signal, no answer, or an answering machine,

By raising or lowering your pledge rate, fulfillment rate, or average gift, a high-quality telephone fundraising program can greatly improve results.

ASSUMPTIONS	
All Donors	30,000
Qualified donors	20,000
Qualified w/phone #	12,000
Completed calls	8,400
Cost	$52,500

PLEDGE RATE		FUFILLMENT RATE	AVERAGE GIFT	NET REVENUE	ABOVE/ BELOW AVERAGE
Effect of change in pledge rate					
Above Average	45%	70%	$36	$42,756	$10,584
Average	40%	70%	$36	$32,172	$0
Below Average	35%	70%	$36	$21,588	($10,584)
Effect of change in fullfillment rate					
Above Average	40%	75%	$36	$38,220	$6,048
Average	40%	70%	$36	$32,172	$0
Below Average	40%	65%	$36	$26,124	($6,048)
Effect of change in average gift					
Above Average	40%	70%	$40	$41,580	$9,408
Average	40%	70%	$36	$32,172	$0
Below Average	40%	70%	$30	$18,060	($14,112)

Skill and experience can pay off in telephone fundraising.

the callers will reach about seventy percent, or 8,400.

- It's reasonable to expect that between thirty and fifty percent of the 8,400 donors you reach will pledge a contribution of a specific amount. (The qualifier is important, because many will also make vague promises or drop hints but not agree to specific pledges. Nonspecific pledges are much less likely to be fulfilled.) In an active donor resolicitation program, a forty percent pledge rate is typical. That means you'll have 3,360 pledges.
- The "fulfillment rate"—the percentage of donors who actually send in checks—may range from less than half to more than one hundred

percent (in which case the number of non-payers is equalled or exceeded by the number of nonspecific pledges that are fulfilled.) For a well-run telephone fundraising program, a seventy percent fulfillment rate is acceptable. For you, this means 2,352 gifts.

- If the average contribution to all your direct mail resolicitations is $30, removing the 10,000 least responsive donors should raise that average by at least ten percent—and the "warmth" and innate persuasiveness of telephone contact should add another ten percent to the average gift. This means an average of about $36 for each of the 2,352 gifts you receive from this telephone fundraising project, or a gross of

$84,672. (Naturally enough, the average gift almost *always* depends on whom you call.)

But don't expect all $85,000 to come in at once. Telephone contact may take time—several weeks, perhaps, to contact all 8,400 donors. Your telephone fundraising firm then has to mail out pledge cards, and you have to wait for the donors to respond. Many don't.

Most programs follow up once or twice by mail and sometimes by phone as well. Generally, seventy to eighty percent of the proceeds from a telephone fundraising program will be received within 120 days of the date of the first contact with donors. The last contributions should be received within 120 days of the date of the last contact.

As you can see, telephone fundraising isn't a quick way to raise a buck.

While the length and character of the script will determine how much time each phone contact requires, it's likely that callers will average anywhere from four to twelve contacts per hour if they're dialing the phones themselves. The median is almost squarely in the middle of that range, or about eight contacts per hour. At that rate, it will take 1,050 hours of calling to complete the job. If the firm is charging you $50 per caller-hour (including direct mail follow-up costs), the cost of the effort will be $52,500. Eventually, you'll net $32,172.

The numbers look a little different if the calling center uses automated, "predictive-dialing" equipment. These computer-driven systems dial the phones and connect callers on-line only after someone has answered on the other end. The net effect is to increase the frequency of voice-to-voice contact, usually to somewhere within the range of eight to twenty contacts per caller-hour. However, service bureaus that operate with such devices tend to charge on a per-contact basis rather than per-hour. As a result, the impact on your bottom line is often about the same.

In either case, the ratio of revenue to cost in this hypothetical project will be about 1.6 to 1. In other words, you won't even double your money. But there are additional benefits:

■ The chances are you'll be getting gifts from many more than the number of donors who would respond to a direct mail appeal.

■ You'll get larger gifts from many of them than they've ever given before by mail.

■ And you'll establish personal contact with more than one-third of your best donors, which will educate them and build their loyalty.

■ ■ ■ ■

In fact, the numbers I've used in this hypothetical example are conservative. A pledge rate of forty-five percent with eighty percent fulfillment and a $40 average gift is by no means out of the question. In this example, that would mean gross revenue of $120,960. You'd turn a profit of $68,460, with a revenue-to-cost ratio of 2.3 to 1. Integrated mail and phone programs commonly achieve even higher ratios.

An especially effective telephone fundraising program—one carefully segmented to deliver the most powerful message to each segment or type of donor—can upgrade the average contribution by more than ten percent. Some programs successfully generate major gifts. Single contributions of $10,000 or more are not unknown. Careful direct mail follow-up can substantially raise fulfillment rates.

The table on page 83 depicts the bottom-line impact of modest increases or decreases in the average contribution, the response rate, and the fulfillment rate—the difference between competent and mediocre telephone fundraising efforts. Professionals in this demanding and highly competitive industry have developed techniques, often proprietary, to improve results as measured by any or all of these important criteria. Performance varies widely.

But, in any case, don't be mesmerized by dollars and cents. Telephone fundraising can play a strategic role for your organization in three ways:

■ By converting many of your one-time "donors" into genuine supporters.

■ By generating real enthusiasm among many of your reliable donors and coaxing them to give much larger gifts.

■ By conveying the message to your supporters in the most intimate way available to you that their support really *matters*.

Fees charged by telephone fundraising firms vary greatly, and each firm seems to have its own peculiar list of inclusions and exclusions from the base rate. They tend to run from about $30 per caller-hour to $70 or more, or—to look at it a different way—from around $3.50 per contact to

$12.00 or more. Experience and levels of talent also vary. Chances are, you'll get what you pay for. You're not likely to find any bargains.

Cost is only one of a great many issues to consider about telephone fundraising. Normally, you can lower the cost by:

- Limiting the duration of the contact (the "script").
- Cheapening the quality of the printed materials sent to those who pledge to contribute.
- Avoiding "lead letters" or postcards to the donors you're going to call.
- Simplifying the methods and terms of collecting payments.

It may not be smart for you to do any of these things.

When you look around the telephone fundraising field, you should also find out whether a firm you're considering is properly registered to do business in the states where your donors live. Regulation of telephone fundraising has become a controversial issue of considerable staying power, and I'm sure you'll agree it's essential to conduct your affairs with scrupulous regard for both legal and ethical standards.

Telephone pledge package

A telephone pledge card package (or gift fulfillment package) may contain several items. On the following three pages are elements of two commonly used formats.

Pages 86 and 87 feature a telephone pledge package containing four items:

- A personalized one-page letter.
- A closed-face #10 carrier envelope (later stamped with a commemorative 29-cent stamp).
- A pre-addressed #9 reply envelope (which also bore a first-class stamp).
- A personalized pledge card or response device, which was originally printed on the same sheet as the matching letter, then cut off. This is a format sometimes known as "slit-and-fold."

The package shown here is a High-Dollar package. Such packages are *not* common. It's the slit-and-fold format that you're likely to see elsewhere.

On page 88 you'll find an example of what we call a "Maybe Letter." Letters like this, often more than one page long, are included in pledge packages to donors who did *not* specify a particular dollar amount. (Many professionals call them "unspecified pledges.")

Some pledge packages contain additional items, such as lift letters, buckslips, stickers, or other front-end premiums.

PARTNERS in CONSERVATION
A SOCIETY OF WORLD WILDLIFE FUND

September 8, 1994

Dr. and Mrs. Jamie Q. Sample
145 Main St
Anytown, New Jersey 07080

Dear Dr. and Mrs. Sample:

Thank you for your pledge of $1000.00 to World Wildlife Fund to renew your membership in Partners in Conservation. Your past generosity and continuing support are greatly appreciated.

With your help, World Wildlife Fund has worked against what seem truly desperate odds for survival of the world's tigers and rhinos, promoted a balanced approach to conservation of key marine species, and built partnerships with local conservation groups and indigenous people in Africa, Asia, and the Americas to promote conservation through education and training programs.

Your renewed membership in Partners in Conservation makes you a champion of critical WWF projects, including those to

- safeguard the fragile desert ecosystems of Namibia - home to desert-adapted elephants, lions, and black rhinos - by working with local communities to find ways to manage natural resources and coexist with wildlife;

- protect the near-pristine temperate forests of the Russian Far East - which harbor a rich array of wildlife including Siberian tigers, leopards, and bears - by halting poaching and habitat destruction, and by working with Russian colleagues to develop a nationwide biodiversity conservation strategy; and

- conserve the Calakmul Biosphere Reserve in Mexico - that supports more than 400 vertebrate species including five species of wild cats - and stem the relentless tide of deforestation that threatens their survival.

Our ultimate success depends on the steadfast commitment of Partners like you. Thank you for your renewed pledge to support World Wildlife Fund and global conservation.

Sincerely,

Kathryn S. Fuller

Kathryn S. Fuller
President

1250 TWENTY-FOURTH STREET, NW   WASHINGTON, DC 20037-1175

recycled paper

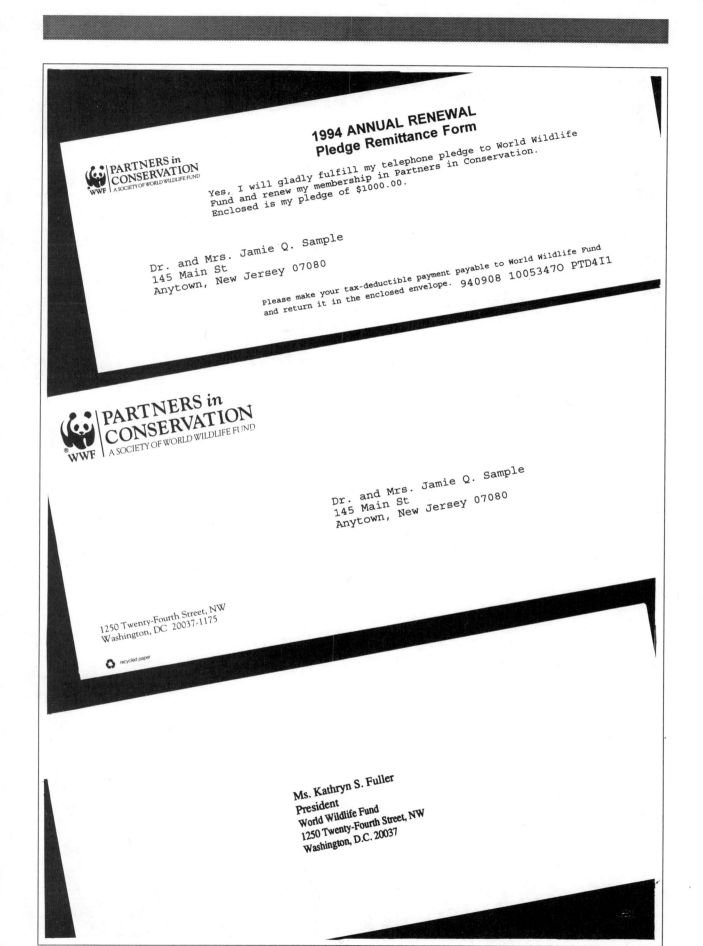

1994 ANNUAL RENEWAL
Pledge Remittance Form

Yes, I will gladly fulfill my telephone pledge to World Wildlife
Fund and renew my membership in Partners in Conservation.
Enclosed is my pledge of $1000.00.

Dr. and Mrs. Jamie Q. Sample
145 Main St
Anytown, New Jersey 07080

Please make your tax-deductible payment payable to World Wildlife Fund
and return it in the enclosed envelope. 940908 10053470 PTD4I1

PARTNERS in CONSERVATION
A SOCIETY OF WORLD WILDLIFE FUND

Dr. and Mrs. Jamie Q. Sample
145 Main St
Anytown, New Jersey 07080

1250 Twenty-Fourth Street, NW
Washington, DC 20037-1175

recycled paper

Ms. Kathryn S. Fuller
President
World Wildlife Fund
1250 Twenty-Fourth Street, NW
Washington, D.C. 20037

The New York Public Library

476 Fifth Avenue, New York, New York, 10018-2788

Dear Friend:

Thank you for taking the time the other night to speak with a representative of The New York Public Library. <u>Your renewed support is critical if the Library is to fulfill its educational mission.</u>

The New York Public Library is the only major research library in the world supported primarily by private funds that is open -- and FREE -- to all people, regardless of where they live, where they work, or what their income. Students, teachers, immigrants, business professionals, writers, artists and casual users all look to the Library every day to get the information they want and need.

It is easy to take this great "People's University" for granted and assume that its doors will always be open and the books and other materials that make up its peerless collections will always be available and in good condition.

But to provide such essential services, <u>the Library must raise over $9 million each year</u> in operating support from the private sector -- from you and thousands of other generous individuals like you who become Friends of the Library!

We need your renewed support -- NOW -- to help the Library <u>maintain its hours of service</u>, <u>provide up-to-date reference materials</u> (many in expensive electronic formats), and <u>hire skilled staff</u> who can help make accessible vital information for all our users.

Please send your membership gift of $35, $50, $100 -- or more -- today! Help keep The New York Public Library one of the premier educational resources of our city and our country.

Sincerely,

Paul LeClerc
President

P.S. The Library's fiscal year ends June 30th and <u>we still need to raise $149,000 to meet our budgeted expenses.</u> Please consider making a contribution TODAY. Your support is urgently needed!

♻ Printed on recycled paper.

six

An inside look at one campaign

TO LAUNCH ITS INITIAL CAMPAIGN for San Francisco-based TURN(Toward Utility Rate Normalization), Mal Warwick & Associates, Inc. designed and produced a mailing in eight parts, or segments. In the following pages, you can see exactly what we mailed.

The campaign illustrated here was conducted in 1989. Why—five years later—am I reproducing the same packages? Two reasons:

PACKAGE	QUANTITY	COST PER PIECE	RESPONSE RATE	NUMBER OF GIFTS
"Maxi-Donor" Year-End Renewal	5,870	$1.99	46.7%	2,737
"Active Donor" Year-End Renewal	12,728	$0.54	20.6%	2,624
Lapsed Donor Reactivation	14,188	$0.44	10.6%	1,497
Acquisition Control Package	130,841	$0.29	2.4%	3,137
Survey Test Package	29,917	$0.29	2.6%	767
Free Sticker Test Package	29,921	$0.33	1.6%	480
Teaser Test Package	29,925	$0.29	1.8%	528
Price Test Package	29,921	$0.29	2.2%	650

TURN's kickoff included four mailings and eight packages.

- First, I'd make only minor changes in these packages if I were asked to mail them again today.
- Second, the acquisition control package we're mailing for TURN to this day is, in all major respects, the same package we mailed in 1989.

All eight package variations were based on a detailed "copy platform"—a "case statement" summarizing the arguments for supporting TURN—that was conceived, edited, and approved by TURN's executive director. TURN dictated every substantive aspect and factual detail of the message, and later edited and approved every word appearing in the eight letters.

Three similar packages were mailed to different segments of TURN's active and lapsed donors—a total of 32,786. At about the same time, we mailed five versions of a donor acquisition package to selected portions of a much larger collection of prospective donor lists. A total of 8,158 inactive and low-dollar TURN donors were included in the prospect pool.

Altogether, there were a quarter-million prospect packages. Of the "Important Notice," the control package, we produced about 130,000. It was the standard against which we tested results for the other four versions. We printed and mailed some 30,000 of each of the four at a unit cost of twenty-nine to thirty-three cents.

While this mailing was an "initial test" for us, it was a continuation of a long-running direct mail fundraising program. We began our work with extensive knowledge of the market, based on TURN's previous mailings. This enabled us to mail a much larger number of letters than is ordinarily the case in an initial test.

Overall, the response rate was 2.2 percent, but it varied from one package to another. The survey version yielded 2.6 percent, the control 2.4 percent, and the other three ranged from 1.6 to 2.2 percent. The average contribution also varied.

Because of TURN's proprietary interests, I can't report here the average gifts received. Take my word for it, though: in this case, it's not valid to conclude that the version with the highest response rate was the most successful.

The results TURN obtained from both prospect and resolicitation packages were extraordinary, running between fifteen and forty percent over projections. The strength of these packages clearly helped explain the excellent results. So,

too, did the long time elapsed since the last previous resolicitation. But more than any other factor, this direct mail success story is due to TURN's remarkable success in battling for the rights of California utility consumers. And it didn't hurt a bit that TURN's founder and then-executive director, Sylvia Siegel, is one of the state's best-known and most beloved consumer advocates, and a wonderfully quotable and colorful person to boot. Direct mail fundraising doesn't operate in a vacuum.

Core Donor year-end renewal

TURN's Core Donors (or Maxi-Donors)—its most loyal, most frequent and most generous contributors—received a high-quality personalized package. This included the items reproduced on pages 91-95:
- A "closed-face" outer envelope (one, that is, without a window).
- A personalized letter and response device.
- A reply envelope bearing a "live" first-class stamp.

Only about eighteen percent of TURN's prime donor list were in this Core Donor group.

We mailed 5,870 of these packages at a cost of about $1.99 apiece. Nearly forty-seven percent of the recipients responded generously. The mailing produced a *very* significant profit.

TURN
Toward Utility Rate Normalization
693 Mission Street
San Francisco, CA 94105

Mr. John Doe
123 Main Street
Anytown, AS 00000

Mr. John Doe
123 Main Street
Anytown, AS 00000

Dear Sylvia,

　　　Yes, I want to help TURN stop the new tricks
the utilities are using to raise my gas, electric
and phone bills. Here's my special, tax-deductible,
year-end contribution to help you fight for fair
utility rates for all Californians in 1989:

[ ] $200   [ ] $1,000   [ ] $_____

I have made my tax-deductible contribution
payable to TURN and I am returning it in the
postage-paid envelope provided.

0200

TURN
Financial Processing Service
2550 Ninth Street, #1038
Berkeley, CA 94710

TURN

Toward Utility Rate Normalization
693 Mission Street
San Francisco, CA 94105

Sylvia M. Siegel
Executive Director

December 22, 1988

Mr. John Doe
123 Main Street
Anytown, AS 00000

Dear Mr. Doe,

What's in store for your natural gas, electricity, and phone bills next year? I'll give you my best forecast in a moment. But first, I want to say a big THANK YOU for your past support of TURN.

Without it, we could never have accomplished all we did in 1988. And <u>what</u> a year 1988 has been!

Your gas, electric, and telephone companies outdid themselves. They dreamed up the most complicated and outlandish schemes yet to get their hands on <u>more</u> of <u>your</u> money while giving you <u>less</u> in return.

TURN beat back those schemes, thanks to your support. TURN's hardworking staff put in overtime to keep OUTRAGEOUS overcharges off your bills:

o   TURN went all the way to Washington, D.C. -- to argue for lower rates on your phone bill before the U.S. House of Representatives Telecommunications and Finance Committee. And TURN joined an appeal of a FCC decision that initiated the access charge scam.

o   TURN went to the state legislature in Sacramento to keep your natural gas bills from going through the roof.

o   And TURN spent weeks on end with the Public Utilities Commission in San Francisco to keep ALL your utility bills down.

Just look at how TURN's hard work (and your support) has paid off. In 1988, we chalked up these important victories:

** TURN got <u>Pacific Bell toll call charges lowered</u> by between <u>5%</u> and <u>32%</u>. And we convinced the PUC to <u>slash AT&T's long-distance rates by 28%</u>. Sprint and MCI slashed their rates similarly.

** TURN successfully opposed a $2 charge for blocking "976" programs from your telephone. Why should you pay to remove an unsolicited service from your telephone?

** TURN stopped a DISGRACEFUL plan to raise your natural gas and electricity rates. It all started when last year's cold winter sent southern California heating bills sky high.

SoCal Gas was giving its big industrial users whopping discounts. Then, it tacked exorbitant charges onto the bills of ordinary households that went over the "baseline rate" in order to finance its giveaways to big users.

Now, the obvious solution to this problem is for SoCal Gas and other California natural gas companies to stop undercharging big customers and stop overcharging small customers. But did they agree to do that? No way.

Instead, they had the gall to go to the state legislature and try to get the baseline rate outlawed. That would have raised your gas and electricity bill.

It would have raised gas and electricity bills for all but the wealthiest Californians.

In the worst case, it could have meant illness or even death for senior citizens, single mothers, and other people who just barely get by. For those who barely manage to pay their winter heat bills, even a few dollars in higher rates can mean catastrophe!

TURN stopped that one in Sacramento. And we'll be there every time the gas and electric companies try these tricks. We'll fight any plan to shift costs from big industrial users onto households like yours.

** Another decisive victory that helped you in 1988 was halting PacBell's abusive marketing practices.

Pacific Bell had been tricking people into ordering services like Call Forwarding and Call Waiting -- even when they didn't want them. Then, the unsuspecting customers paid for these services every month, even if they NEVER used them. But the charge was hidden on the bill!

Because TURN and other consumer advocates blew the whistle on this swindle, the PUC made PacBell stop. Even more, we won refunds for the people who were cheated ($27 million so far). And we won a ruling that forced PacBell to set up a $16.5 million trust fund to educate the public about their rights as telephone consumers.

There's no mystery about how TURN wins all these victories. It's just plain old hard work. We always have justice on our side. But we have to sort through mountains of boring documents and check endless columns of figures to prove it.

The phone, gas, and electric companies try to make it all so complicated, ordinary folks can't understand what they're up to.

That's why ordinary Californians need TURN. We argue on your behalf every day of the year. To make sure you don't pay one penny more than you should.

Now back to my forecast for your bills in 1989. Just take a look at what's in store:

(1) California's phone, natural gas, and electricity companies are making a big push for deregulation.

This would mean they could raise your bills as high as they want -- and you would have nowhere to turn. The Public Utilities Commission would no longer provide a forum for stopping their rate hikes. No one would stop them.

Even worse, nothing would stop the utilities investing the proceeds from your electric bill (or your gas or phone bill) in anything they wanted. Risky mergers. Foreign real estate. Questionable loans. Anything.

And if their risky investments hurt their credit rating, they could get back the higher finance costs they'd have to pay, simply by upping the charges on your phone, gas, or electric bill.

This is clearly outrageous. TURN is pledged to stop it, but it will be a hard fight. I ask for your support once again. I assure you that if we have it, we will win.

(2) The second big fight in 1989 will be over the Diablo Canyon Nuclear Power Plant. PG&E is trying to sock its customers with the $5.8 billion the plant cost. PG&E ran up big bills on engineering mistakes and design flaws building this costly boondoggle.

TURN insists that PG&E's stockholders should bear the cost. We've been fighting this one for a long time. The Public Utilities Commission is exhausted from wading through PG&E's piles of paper. (One set of arguments was so big, PG&E had to use a Bekins moving van to deliver it!)

The PUC is trying to cut a deal. But TURN says NO DEAL!

This deal will mean higher electric bills for the next 30 years! If the PUC makes this deal, TURN is ready to fight it all the way to the U.S. Supreme Court!

(3) We're also out to win <u>metropolitan</u> <u>phone</u> <u>rates</u> for you. This will mean no more of those "zone" charges when you call nearby communities.

<u>Your</u> <u>basic</u> <u>phone</u> <u>rate</u> <u>should</u> <u>cover</u> <u>your</u> <u>entire</u> <u>metropolitan</u> <u>area</u>. And you should get that service for the same basic rate you pay now -- or even lower.

So, what's going to happen to your utility bills next year? Just as we won in 1988, TURN can win in 1989. And if we do, <u>we'll</u> <u>save</u> <u>you</u> <u>money</u> <u>on</u> <u>your</u> <u>phone</u>, <u>gas</u>, <u>and</u> <u>electric</u> <u>bills</u>. But we rely on your support to keep up the fight.

The utilities never contribute a dime to keep TURN alive. And big businesses don't support us, either. We've stopped <u>them</u> too many times from getting lavish discounts at <u>your</u> expense.

<u>We're</u> <u>counting</u> <u>on</u> <u>support</u> <u>from</u> <u>you</u>. Please make a special, year-end contribution to help TURN gear up to save you money in 1989. Send back your contribution with your personal reply form in the postage-paid reply envelope enclosed.

Your tax-deductible donation will go a long way. Because at TURN, we make every penny count.

We don't have fancy offices. Our staff of experts could get more than double the salaries they earn at TURN if they went over to the other side. But they'll never do that.

We're dedicated to making sure that you -- and other California consumers -- get a fair shake. In 1989, just like in 1988, just like every year since 1973 -- TURN will be there.

TURN has saved the average Californian hundreds of dollars over the years. But the natural gas, electricity, and phone companies are poised with a whole bag of new tricks, waiting to snatch it all back and then some. They'll do it, too, if they get the chance.

Please lend your support to make sure they don't. Because if you keep TURN there, you can bet your bottom dollar that your gas, electric, and phone companies won't get the chance to rip you off.

Sincerely,

Sylvia M. Siegel

Sylvia M. Siegel
Executive Director

P.S. The phone, gas, and electric companies are pushing hard for deregulation as soon as possible. If they win, they'll be able to raise your bills <u>as</u> <u>high</u> <u>as</u> <u>they</u> <u>like</u>, <u>with</u> <u>NO</u> <u>limit</u>. TURN needs your contribution right now to make sure we have the resources to stop them. So I ask you, please, to send your contribution <u>within</u> <u>the</u> <u>next</u> <u>10</u> <u>days</u>.

Sylvia M. Siegel

'f you know what will happen to your utility bills in 1989?

'URN
ward Utility Rate Normalization
3 Mission Street
n Francisco, CA 94105

Dear Sylvia,

Yes, I want to help TURN stop the new tricks the utilities are using to raise my gas, electric and phone bills. Here's my special, tax-deductible, year-end contribution to help you fight for fair utility rates for all Californians in 1989:

☐ $25 ☐ $35 ☐ $50 ☐ $75 ☐ $100 ☐ $250 ☐ $____

SAMPLE
Mr. John Doe
123 Any Street
Any Town, AS 00000

"I'm not going to let those utilities rip you off in 1989."

Please make your check payable to **TURN.** Thank you.

Active Donor year-end renewal

Thirty-nine percent of TURNs' donors received a "generic" (non-personalized) version of the Core Donor appeal. In other words, the salutation read "Dear Friend" rather than using the donor's name. The text of the letter was virtually identical except on the fourth page (see opposite), but the message was packaged far less expensively. We affixed a "Cheshire" mailing label to a pre-printed reply device and mailed it in a window carrier along with a Business Reply Envelope, all of which you can see above.

We mailed 12,728 of these packages costing about fifty-four cents each. A heartening twenty percent responded with gifts, adding substantially to TURN's net profit from the project as a whole.

Page 4

(3) We're also out to win <u>metropolitan phone rates</u> for you. This will mean no more of those "zone" charges when you call nearby communities.

<u>Your basic phone rate should cover your entire metropolitan area</u>. And you should get that service for the same basic rate you pay now -- or even lower.

So, what's going to happen to your utility bills next year? Just as we won in 1988, TURN can win in 1989. And if we do, <u>we'll save you money on your phone, gas, and electric bills</u>. But we rely on your support to keep up the fight.

The utilities never contribute a dime to keep TURN alive. And big businesses don't support us, either. We've stopped <u>them</u> too many times from getting lavish discounts at <u>your</u> expense.

<u>We're counting on support from you</u>. Please make a special, year-end contribution to help TURN gear up to save you money in 1989. Your tax-deductible donation of $20, $35, $50, $75, or $100 will go a long way. Because at TURN, we make every penny count.

We don't have fancy offices. Our staff of experts could get more than double the salaries they earn at TURN if they went over to the other side. But they'll never do that.

We're dedicated to making sure that you -- and other California consumers -- get a fair shake. In 1989, just like in 1988, just like every year since 1973 -- TURN will be there.

TURN has saved the average Californian hundreds of dollars over the years. But the natural gas, electricity, and phone companies are poised with a whole bag of new tricks, waiting to snatch it all back and then some. They'll do it, too, if they get the chance.

Please lend your support to make sure they don't. Because if you keep TURN there, you can bet your bottom dollar that your gas, electric, and phone companies won't get the chance to rip you off.

Sincerely,

Sylvia M. Siegel

Sylvia M. Siegel
Executive Director

P.S. The phone, gas, and electric companies are pushing hard for deregulation starting as soon as possible. If they win, they'll be able to raise your bills <u>as high as they like</u>, <u>with NO limit</u>. TURN needs your contribution right now to make sure we have the resources to stop them. So I ask you, please, to send your contribution <u>within the next 10 days</u>.

Lapsed Donor reactivation

To "reactivate" lapsed donors—those forty-three percent of TURN supporters who hadn't sent contributions in more than eighteen months—we affixed a handwritten note to the letter we'd written for active supporters. The note read as follows:

Here's your copy of a letter I sent to all our current supporters.

—Sylvia

We added a combined "Strategy Survey" and contribution form along with a special note from Sylvia Siegel. (See below and opposite.) Then we wrapped these items in the same window carrier we'd printed for active donors. The whole package cost about forty-four cents per piece.

Typically, response is poor to lapsed donor appeals of this type. But nearly eleven percent of the 14,188 who received these packages returned gifts to TURN.

From the desk of
Sylvia M. Siegel

Dear Friend,

In the past, you supported TURN when we really needed it. Without you, TURN wouldn't have been able to save Californians over $7 billion on phone, electricity and natural gas bills.

But we haven't heard from you in a long time now.

I'm enclosing a copy of a letter I sent all TURN's current supporters. I want to let you in, too, on what we've accomplished in 1988. The utility companies came close to outright gouging on your bills. And TURN stopped them in the nick of time.

But the utilities are already at work on new scams for 1989. And it doesn't take a crystal ball to see that if TURN isn't there to fight them, your rates will go up.

Please, read the whole story in the enclosed letter. When you do, you'll see TURN really needs old friends like you more than ever now. Please give careful consideration to supporting TURN once again.

Sincerely,

Sylvia M. Siegel

Sylvia M. Siegel

P.S. One thing we've really missed are your ideas. Now, I need your help to determine TURN's strategy for next year. Won't you please take a few moments to fill out the special "1989 TURN Strategy Survey" I've prepared for you?

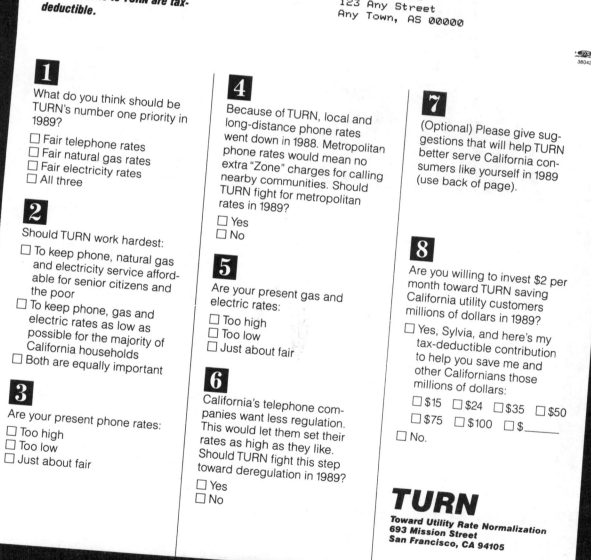

1989 TURN Strategy Survey

NUMBER: C1039Z   PREPARED FOR:

Please return this 1989 TURN Strategy Survey along with your check in the enclosed envelope. Make checks payable to TURN. Contributions to TURN are tax-deductible.

SAMPLE
Mr. John Doe
123 Any Street
Any Town, AS 00000

38042

1

What do you think should be TURN's number one priority in 1989?

☐ Fair telephone rates
☐ Fair natural gas rates
☐ Fair electricity rates
☐ All three

2

Should TURN work hardest:

☐ To keep phone, natural gas and electricity service affordable for senior citizens and the poor
☐ To keep phone, gas and electric rates as low as possible for the majority of California households
☐ Both are equally important

3

Are your present phone rates:

☐ Too high
☐ Too low
☐ Just about fair

4

Because of TURN, local and long-distance phone rates went down in 1988. Metropolitan phone rates would mean no extra "Zone" charges for calling nearby communities. Should TURN fight for metropolitan rates in 1989?

☐ Yes
☐ No

5

Are your present gas and electric rates:

☐ Too high
☐ Too low
☐ Just about fair

6

California's telephone companies want less regulation. This would let them set their rates as high as they like. Should TURN fight this step toward deregulation in 1989?

☐ Yes
☐ No

7

(Optional) Please give suggestions that will help TURN better serve California consumers like yourself in 1989 (use back of page).

8

Are you willing to invest $2 per month toward TURN saving California utility customers millions of dollars in 1989?

☐ Yes, Sylvia, and here's my tax-deductible contribution to help you save me and other Californians those millions of dollars:

☐ $15 ☐ $24 ☐ $35 ☐ $50
☐ $75 ☐ $100 ☐ $_____
☐ No.

TURN

**Toward Utility Rate Normalization
693 Mission Street
San Francisco, CA 94105**

San Francisco Examiner

Professional underdog

THE PILES OF paper would have gladdened any pack rat's heart, but Sylvia Siegel said things weren't quite as chaotic as usual.

"I've tried to clean up a little," she said, "because '60 Minutes' has been following me around."

Siegel is a short, plump, white-haired woman who says she's old enough to retire but won't go further than that ("My age is nobody's damned business").

Once in awhile, you can find her in her Mill Valley home, making chopped liver. Most of the time you can find her in one of three other places: her none-too-fancy office on Mission Street, working the phones or those stacks of stuff; a courtroom or a hearing room, taking on PG&E or Pacific Bell; or out among the people, ringing doorbells, raising money, spreading the word.

Siegel is a consumer activist, the executive director of Toward Utility Rate Normalization (TURN), which for the last 10 years plus has fought hard and with surprising effectiveness for the little guy and the middle-sized guy.

It's estimated that Siegel and her staff, which now includes three lawyers, an educational outreach worker, a secretary and five to 10 canvassers who go door to door passing out information and raising funds, have saved Californians more than $7 billion in gas, electrical and phone rates.

SIEGEL IS not a lawyer, but she's mastered the highly complex ways of utility regulation to the point where she's won many significant victories in the courts and before the state Public Utilities Commission.

Several years ago, Siegel helped force the utilities to establish "life-line" rates — low-cost, basic service for the elderly and the poor.

Recently, TURN won the right (through the PUC) to insert promotional and fund-raising mailing into PG&E bills and is seeking the same access to telephone bills.

At the same time, Siegel and her group are battling hard to cut back Pacific Bell's $446 million rate increase.

"We're carrying a new briefcase every day," she says. "We usually have four or five major cases going on at a time. I don't look at my calendar much anymore. It just makes me tired."

Siegel has been involved in unusual pursuits most of her life.

"I knew I wasn't destined for any ordinary pursuit," she says. "I'm a Taurus. I'm persistent. I have no patience with anything dull."

Acquisition packages: the control

Prospective TURN donors received one of five Cheshire-label packages as a result of our effort to determine the most cost-effective donor acquisition strategy. The only common elements in all five packages were a news clipping and a Business Reply Envelope. Other elements varied from one package to another.

The "control" package, including the full text of the letter, is reproduced above and on the next four pages.

TURN

Toward Utility Rate Normalization
693 Mission Street
San Francisco, CA 94105

Sylvia M. Siegel
Executive Director

Dear Friend,

What's in store for your natural gas, electricity, and phone bills next year? I'll give you my best forecast in a moment. But first, I want to say a big THANK YOU for your past support of TURN.

Without it, we could never have accomplished all we did in 1988. And _what_ a year 1988 has been!

Your gas, electric, and telephone companies outdid themselves. They dreamed up the most complicated and outlandish schemes yet to get their hands on _more_ of _your_ money while giving you _less_ in return.

TURN beat back those schemes, thanks to your support. TURN's hardworking staff put in overtime to keep OUTRAGEOUS overcharges off your bills:

o   TURN went all the way to Washington, D.C. -- to argue for lower rates on your phone bill before the U.S. House of Representatives Telecommunications and Finance Committee. And TURN joined an appeal of a FCC decision that initiated the access charge scam.

o   TURN went to the state legislature in Sacramento to keep your natural gas bills from going through the roof.

o   And TURN spent weeks on end with the Public Utilities Commission in San Francisco to keep ALL your utility bills down.

Just look at how TURN's hard work (and your support) has paid off. In 1988, we chalked up these important victories:

** TURN got _Pacific Bell_ _toll_ _call_ _charges_ _lowered_ _by_ _between_ _5%_ _and_ _32%_. And we convinced the PUC to _slash_ _AT&T's_ _long-distance_ _rates_ _by_ _28%_. Sprint and MCI slashed their rates similarly.

38029

** TURN successfully opposed a $2 charge for blocking "976" programs from your telephone. Why should you pay to remove an unsolicited service from your telephone?

** TURN stopped a DISGRACEFUL plan to raise your natural gas and electricity rates. It all started when last year's cold winter sent southern California heating bills sky high.

SoCal Gas was giving its big industrial users whopping discounts. Then, it tacked exorbitant charges onto the bills of ordinary households that went over the "baseline rate" in order to finance its giveaways to big users.

Now, the obvious solution to this problem is for SoCal Gas and other California natural gas companies to <u>stop undercharging</u> <u>big customers</u> <u>and stop overcharging small customers</u>. But did they agree to do that? No way.

Instead, they had the gall to go to the state legislature and try to get the <u>baseline rate outlawed</u>. That would have raised <u>your</u> gas and electricity bill.

It would have raised gas and electricity bills for <u>all</u> but the <u>wealthiest</u> Californians.

In the worst case, it could have meant illness or even death for senior citizens, single mothers, and other people who just barely get by. For those who barely manage to pay their winter heat bills, even a few dollars in higher rates can mean catastrophe!

TURN stopped that one in Sacramento. And we'll be there <u>every time</u> the gas and electric companies try these tricks. We'll fight <u>any</u> plan to shift costs from big industrial users onto households like yours.

** Another decisive victory that helped you in 1988 was <u>halting PacBell's abusive marketing practices</u>.

Pacific Bell had been tricking people into ordering services like Call Forwarding and Call Waiting -- even when they didn't want them. Then, the unsuspecting customers paid for these services <u>every month</u>, even if they NEVER used them. But the charge was hidden on the bill!

Because TURN and other consumer advocates blew the whistle on this swindle, the PUC made PacBell stop. Even more, we won <u>refunds</u> for the people who were cheated ($27 million so far). And we won a ruling that forced PacBell to set up a $16.5 million trust fund to educate the public about their <u>rights as telephone</u> <u>consumers</u>.

There's no mystery about how TURN wins all these victories. It's just plain old hard work. We always have justice on our side. But we have to sort through mountains of boring documents and check endless columns of figures to prove it.

The phone, gas, and electric companies try to make it all so complicated, ordinary folks can't understand what they're up to.

That's why ordinary Californians need TURN. We argue on your behalf every day of the year. To make sure you don't pay one penny more than you should.

Now back to my forecast for your bills in 1989. Just take a look at what's in store:

(1) California's phone, natural gas, and electricity companies are making a big push for deregulation.

This would mean they could raise your bills as high as they want -- and you would have nowhere to turn. The Public Utilities Commission would no longer provide a forum for stopping their rate hikes. No one would stop them.

Even worse, nothing would stop the utilities investing the proceeds from your electric bill (or your gas or phone bill) in anything they wanted. Risky mergers. Foreign real estate. Questionable loans. Anything.

And if their risky investments hurt their credit rating, they could get back the higher finance costs they'd have to pay, simply by upping the charges on your phone, gas, or electric bill.

This is clearly outrageous. TURN is pledged to stop it, but it will be a hard fight. I ask for your support once again. I assure you that if we have it, we will win.

(2) The second big fight in 1989 will be over the Diablo Canyon Nuclear Power Plant. PG&E is trying to sock its customers with the $5.8 billion the plant cost. PG&E ran up big bills on engineering mistakes and design flaws building this costly boondoggle.

TURN insists that PG&E's stockholders should bear the cost. We've been fighting this one for a long time. The Public Utilities Commission is exhausted from wading through PG&E's piles of paper. (One set of arguments was so big, PG&E had to use a Bekins moving van to deliver it!)

The PUC is trying to cut a deal. But TURN says NO DEAL!

This deal will mean higher electric bills for the next 30 years! If the PUC makes this deal, TURN is ready to fight it all the way to the U.S. Supreme Court!

(3) We're also out to win <u>metropolitan phone rates</u> for you. This will mean no more of those "zone" charges when you call nearby communities.

<u>Your basic phone rate should cover your entire metropolitan area</u>. And you should get that service for the same basic rate you pay now -- or even lower.

So, what's going to happen to your utility bills next year? Just as we won in 1988, TURN can win in 1989. And if we do, <u>we'll save you money on your phone, gas, and electric bills</u>. But we rely on your support to keep up the fight.

The utilities never contribute a dime to keep TURN alive. And big businesses don't support us, either. We've stopped <u>them</u> too many times from getting lavish discounts at <u>your</u> expense.

<u>We're counting on support from you</u>. Please make a special, year-end contribution to help TURN gear up to save you money in 1989. Your tax-deductible donation of $20, $35, $50, $75, or $100 will go a long way. Because at TURN, we make every penny count.

We don't have fancy offices. Our staff of experts could get more than double the salaries they earn at TURN if they went over to the other side. But they'll never do that.

We're dedicated to making sure that you -- and other California consumers -- get a fair shake. In 1989, just like in 1988, just like every year since 1973 -- TURN will be there.

TURN has saved the average Californian hundreds of dollars over the years. But the natural gas, electricity, and phone companies are poised with a whole bag of new tricks, waiting to snatch it all back and then some. They'll do it, too, if they get the chance.

Please lend your support to make sure they don't. Because if you keep TURN there, you can bet your bottom dollar that your gas, electric, and phone companies won't get the chance to rip you off.

Sincerely,

Sylvia M. Siegel

Sylvia M. Siegel
Executive Director

P.S. The phone, gas, and electric companies are pushing hard for deregulation starting as soon as possible. If they win, they'll be able to raise your bills <u>as high as they like</u>, <u>with NO limit</u>. TURN needs your contribution right now to make sure we have the resources to stop them. So I ask you, please, to send your contribution <u>within the next 10 days</u>.

Acquisition packages: the survey test

One of the three test versions of the TURN acquisition package contained a "California Telephone Rate Customer Survey" integrated into the reply device, along with the control letter, its text slightly altered. On the first page, the following copy was added:

> If I have hard evidence that informed Californians are against this scam, it will help me win. That's why I'm asking you, after you read this letter, to <u>complete the California Telephone Rate Customer Survey I've enclosed</u>.

The letter also closed with a new postscript:

> I really need your opinions on the enclosed survey to back up my arguments when I go before the Public Utilities Commission. Please give a few minutes of your time to fill it out and return it today—so we have it before the hearings start. You'll be helping save yourself and other Californians millions of dollars.

As with the other three acquisition test packages, the news clipping and the Business Reply Envelope used in the control package were also present. See below and the next page for the carrier and the two sides of the Survey.

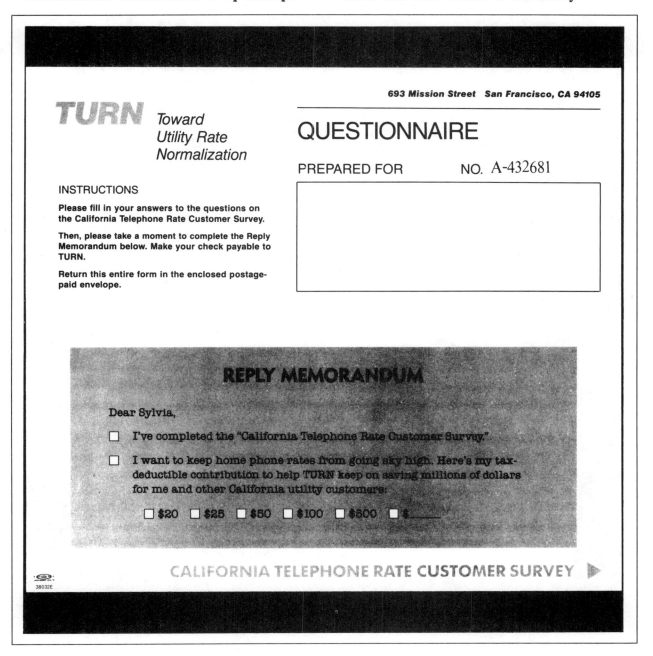

CALIFORNIA TELEPHONE RATE CUSTOMER SURVEY

 1 Pacific Bell should be required to refund the $700 million (an average of $70 for each of us) that they overcharged residential customers last year.

☐ Agree
☐ Disagree

 2 When phone company costs drop, as they have in recent years, raising rates for residential customers is outrageous. Lower costs to the phone company should be passed on to us.

☐ Agree
☐ Disagree

 3 Residential and small business phone users should not have to pay more so Pacific Bell and General Telephone can invest billions in fancy high-tech services for big business.

☐ Agree
☐ Disagree

 4 Local phone rates should cover the whole metropolitan area for the price we pay now—or lower. Zone charges should be discontinued.

☐ Agree
☐ Disagree

 5 It's dangerous for the government to stop regulating phone companies. If they're allowed to set their own rates, our phone bills could go sky high.

☐ Agree
☐ Disagree

If you agree with me on at least three out of these five questions, please join me in fighting the phone companies' exorbitant price hikes. Remember, the money we save will be your own. Sylvia M Siegel

12-5-88

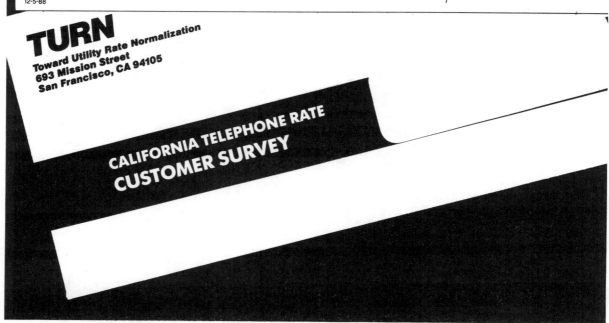

TURN
Toward Utility Rate Normalization
693 Mission Street
San Francisco, CA 94105

CALIFORNIA TELEPHONE RATE
CUSTOMER SURVEY

Acquisition packages: the sticker test

To one test version, we added a sheet of eight "peel-off" stickers. The stickers, the distinctive envelope we mailed them in, and the response device are all pictured. The letter, the news clip-ping, and the Business Reply Envelope were all identical to those included in the control package.

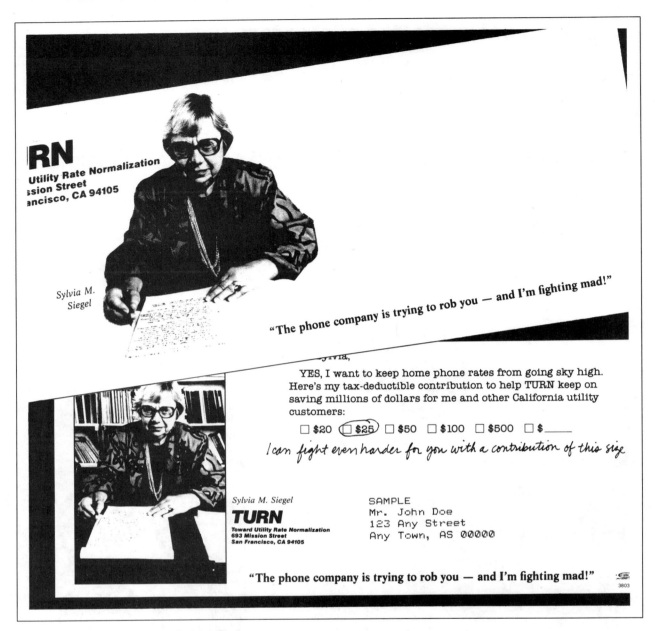

"The phone company is trying to rob you — and I'm fighting mad!"

Sylvia,

YES, I want to keep home phone rates from going sky high. Here's my tax-deductible contribution to help TURN keep on saving millions of dollars for me and other California utility customers:

☐ $20 ⬭ $25 ☐ $50 ☐ $100 ☐ $500 ☐ $____

I can fight even harder for you with a contribution of this size

Sylvia M. Siegel

TURN
Toward Utility Rate Normalization
693 Mission Street
San Francisco, CA 94105

SAMPLE
Mr. John Doe
123 Any Street
Any Town, AS 00000

"The phone company is trying to rob you — and I'm fighting mad!"

3803

Acquisition packages: the teaser test

Yet another TURN acquisition test package used an outer envelope with a photo and distinctive "teaser" copy. The envelope is pictured here, along with the response device it contained. All other elements of this package—the letter, news clipping, and Business Reply Envelope—were identical to those of the control package.

Acquisition packages: the price test

In the fifth version of our initial donor prospecting test for TURN, we suggested a $15 minimum gift instead of a $20 minimum, as on the other four versions. The suggested minimum gift appeared on the response device (see below) as well as on the fourth page of the control letter. In all other respects, this version was identical to the control package.

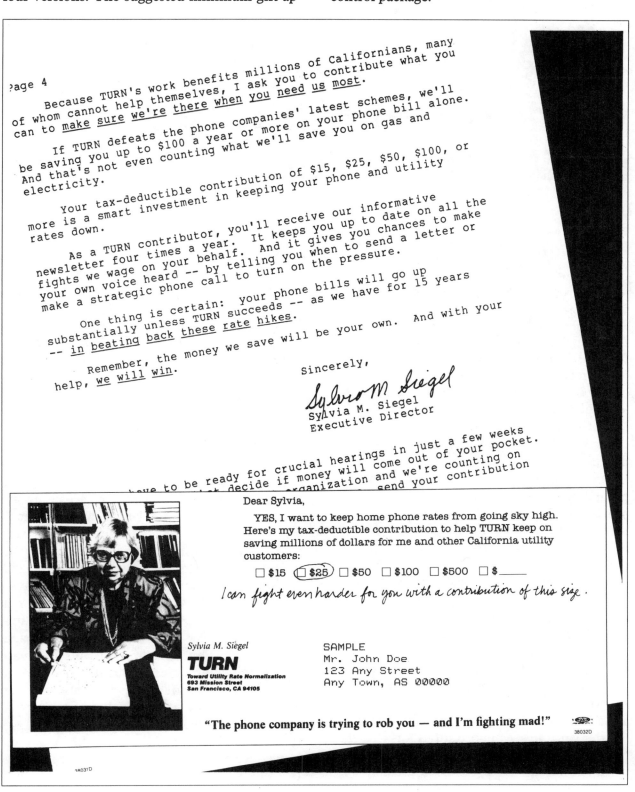

Page 4

Because TURN's work benefits millions of Californians, many of whom cannot help themselves, I ask you to contribute what you can to make sure we're there when you need us most.

If TURN defeats the phone companies' latest schemes, we'll be saving you up to $100 a year or more on your phone bill alone. And that's not even counting what we'll save you on gas and electricity.

Your tax-deductible contribution of $15, $25, $50, $100, or more is a smart investment in keeping your phone and utility rates down.

As a TURN contributor, you'll receive our informative newsletter four times a year. It keeps you up to date on all the fights we wage on your behalf. And it gives you chances to make your own voice heard -- by telling you when to send a letter or make a strategic phone call to turn on the pressure.

One thing is certain: your phone bills will go up substantially unless TURN succeeds -- as we have for 15 years -- in beating back these rate hikes.

Remember, the money we save will be your own. And with your help, we will win.

Sincerely,

Sylvia M. Siegel

Sylvia M. Siegel
Executive Director

have to be ready for crucial hearings in just a few weeks
decide if money will come out of your pocket.
organization and we're counting on
send your contribution

Dear Sylvia,

YES, I want to keep home phone rates from going sky high. Here's my tax-deductible contribution to help TURN keep on saving millions of dollars for me and other California utility customers:

☐ $15   ☐ $25   ☐ $50   ☐ $100   ☐ $500   ☐ $____

I can fight even harder for you with a contribution of this size.

Sylvia M. Siegel

TURN
Toward Utility Rate Normalization
693 Mission Street
San Francisco, CA 94105

SAMPLE
Mr. John Doe
123 Any Street
Any Town, AS 00000

"The phone company is trying to rob you — and I'm fighting mad!"

seven

Working with a direct mail consultant

In-house versus outside management

ADMIT IT: I'M BIASED. As a direct mail fundraising consultant, both self-interest and experience lead me to believe you'd probably be well advised to hire a consultant to help you launch and manage your direct mail fundraising program.

I've made every effort in this book to explain clearly how our business is conducted. Nonetheless, you can see it's very complicated and makes lots of demands on your time and managerial expertise. Chances are, you'll need help—a great deal of it.

Too often, I've seen direct mail fundraising programs that are managed in-house by nonprofit organizations fail to realize their full potential for the following reasons:

- Because staff was distracted by other priorities
- Because they lacked the time or resources to meet maildates on a consistent basis, month after month
- Because the attitudes they conveyed in their mailings were parochial, overly self-serving, or simply uninteresting
- Because they didn't have the depth and scope of experience to know how to respond quickly when creative challenges arose
- Because they just didn't have the breadth of experience to see opportunities for what they were, or to know what to do about them when they surfaced

Frequently, these organizations chose to manage their programs in-house either because they wanted to save money or because they felt they knew better than anyone else how best to present themselves to the world. In most circumstances, neither reason holds water.

The "savings" from in-house management are often illusory. Even if returns on individual mailings are as good as any consultant might obtain, an in-house organization rarely can achieve the consistency and frequency of a mailing schedule managed by outside professionals.

A nonprofit organization rarely has the full range of skills and resources necessary to survive in the Darwinian marketplace of charitable fundraising. Marketing for nonprofits demands a lot more than an intimate understanding of your organization and its work. It's not enough to tell the world what you need. You have to convey your message—cost-effectively—in a way that connects on a visceral level with your constituents and *motivates* them to act, generously and immediately. This calls for a special set of marketing and communications skills that are not common in nonprofit managers. It also calls for an ability to work with specialized suppliers or vendors: a network of list brokers, printers, lettershops, and other vendors that will enable you to produce your mailings on time, and cost-effectively.

Also, nowadays, the difference between success or failure in a mailing can result from very subtle changes in list selection, copy, design, packaging, or timing. Any organization's competitive advantage in direct mail lies on the margins—in very small numbers. For example:

- Lowering the printing cost by two cents per package ($20 per thousand packages) could allow you to mail a million donor acquisition letters—and recruit ten thousand new members—instead of mailing 100,000 and generating only a couple of thousand gifts. (How? Because that many more lists would become cost-effective to mail at the lower cost.) A consultant's clout with printers could make that much difference in the price.

- Mailing eight donor resolicitation letters next year instead of six could increase your organization's net direct mail revenue by twelve or fifteen percent. If your staff is stretched thin, a consultant's attention to the mailing schedule could make the difference.

- Enhancements in copy and design derived from experience with many other nonprofit groups could lift the response rate in each of your donor resolicitations from five percent to eight or ten percent. When the year's at an end, you could find yourself with an active donor base that is twenty or thirty percent larger.

Differences of this magnitude could make or break your strategic plan.

With all this said, however, some organizations are better off managing their programs in-house. This may be the case for your group under the following circumstances:

- If your annual budget is less than $100,000, you're unlikely to be able to afford professional help on a continuing basis.

- If your constituency or market is too small to permit aggressive donor acquisition by mail, you're unlikely to gain enough benefit from an ongoing relationship with a consultant.

- If you've been in the mails for years and your strategy calls for a modest, continuing program along well-established lines that your staff is competent to handle, chances are slim that you'll need anything more than copywriting, technical assistance, or occasional advice.

- If you're on the other end of the spectrum and your direct mail fundraising program is so large and lucrative that you can afford to hire a staff of full-time, top-flight fundraising professionals, you're probably right to handle the job in-house. With several hundred thousand donors and a budget in excess of $20 million, that might be the case. However, if you've gotten that far, you've probably long since figured out that you benefit from hiring not just one but perhaps several outside consultants to provide a steady stream of new ideas and to keep your staff on their toes.

While neither the very biggest nor the smallest organizations may need outsiders to manage their direct mail programs, most of the rest probably do. Chances are, that includes you.

Here, then, are a few guidelines to observe as you look around in search of a direct mail fundraising firm that's right for you.

Selecting the right consultant

There's no license required to hang out a shingle as a direct mail fundraising consultant. There's no test to pass, no certification procedure. And you won't find many of us in the Yellow Pages.

However, there is a national organization that has established a code of ethics for the profession and a mechanism to enforce it. We're called the Association of Direct Response Fundraising Counsel (ADRFCO). The approximately fifty member agencies are located throughout the United States and include most of the major reputable firms in the country. Our clients include more than 600 nonprofit organizations, including many of the nation's biggest and most visible charities. For a listing of members and other information, free of charge, phone (202) 347-0929 or write:

ADRFCO
1319 F Street, N.W.
Suite 300
Washington, DC 20004

A great many of the companies that offer direct mail management, creative, or consulting services to nonprofit organizations are engaged in some *other* business—as printers, computer service bureaus, advertising agencies, list brokers, public relations consultants, or design firms. By and large, with some very notable exceptions, the quality of service offered by these groups is low. Often it's "free"—and in some cases that's exactly what it's worth.

There is also an uncounted number of solo consultants serving one or a few clients, with little or no staff. In a few cases, they're refugees from the constraints imposed by their earlier jobs at larger firms and may offer a range of previous experience. Most, however, gained their principal experience in one direct mail fundraising program, typically as staff for a nonprofit organization, or in commercial direct response marketing. These consultants may offer services ranging from copywriting alone, to full-service management and consulting, to data entry. Some are brilliant fundraisers, but skill levels vary widely among the solo consultants.

Among the dozens of established consulting firms—only a handful of which are more than fifteen years old—the level of skill and breadth of experience also vary. Some work exclusively for nonprofit or political clients. Many pay the bills by taking commercial assignments (for which fees are typically much higher). Some work with a broad range of clients, while others emphasize one or a few special markets or issues. Some have clients nationwide, but others stick to their own regions. Most serve fewer than a dozen organizations at any one time. In most cases, the total staff numbers twenty persons or less.

With such a variety of choices, then, how can you select the consultant that's right for your organization?

As you start the process, you're likely to rely heavily on what you can learn of the firms' reputations and experience. Some may clearly be unsuitable because their track record is unimpressive or is based on issues and organizations that seem irrelevant. Others may clearly be inadequate to the task of meeting your diverse needs. That will help you narrow the field down to a manageable number of three or four prospects. But then the choice is likely to get tougher.

You might start by requesting sample mailing packages from each of the finalists—and then read them. You'll learn a lot. (If they won't send samples, you'll learn something from that, too.)

Naturally, you should also ask for references, or a client list, or both. If you follow up with phone calls to the consultant's references, you'll gain insight that will serve you well whether or not you choose to work with the firm.

But, even after all that, you may still face a difficult choice. Here are the real issues to consider at that point:

- *Understanding*—Do you and the consultant speak the same language? Regardless of whether the firm has direct experience with the issues your organization addresses, do you believe the consulting staff understands what you're about and the values that motivate your constituents? Will they be able to present your programs in fundraising appeals that are honest, accurate, and effective?

- *Range of services*—Does the consultant have the experience and the resources to do the whole job, and do it right? If a firm doesn't itself offer all the services you need, does it have well-established relationships with others who do?

- *Contract terms*—Is the consultant offering attractive financial incentives—such as capital to finance your program or a "guarantee" that you'll make a profit—or offering to accept only a percentage of the returns in compensation? Any or all of these incentive arrangements may be legitimate, but they bear an extra-careful look. They're illegal in many states and are commonly used by crooks. (There are a few such people in the direct mail field, as there are in any other!) And financial incentives may pose problems with the U.S. Postal Service and the Internal Revenue Service.

- *Creativity*—Will the consultant create specially tailored packages for your direct mail fundraising program—or apply formulas (and recycle packages) that have proven successful for other organizations? Winning formulas on which successful agencies have been built include such things as sweepstakes offers and extremely inexpensive prospect package formats. There's no such thing as a "right" or a "wrong" way to look at this question, but it's important stylistically and it may have financial implications. To launch a sweepstakes or use some other tested but controversial formula may be cost-effective, but it may also undermine your support from your board or major funders—or even risk the ire of regulatory authorities. Just be sure you know what you're getting into.

- *Decision-making*—Who will make the key creative and financial decisions—you or the consultant? Does the firm want you to write a check and leave them alone? Or will you be entering into what is effectively a partnership, with the firm making recommendations and you or your staff making the real decisions at every crucial point along the way?

- *Accessibility*—Just because a firm is located in your city doesn't mean you'll get the attention you deserve. Regardless of geographic location, are you convinced the consultant will be available to answer your questions and address your concerns in a timely fashion? Will you get service—or a runaround? Will your telephone calls be answered? Will you have opportunities for periodic strategy and creative meetings?

- *Compensation*—Aside from the management or consulting fees the firm will charge you, what other fees will you be paying? Will the consultant mark up printing and other vendor bills, receive all the list rental revenue, or even receive title to your donor or membership list? The proposed "fees" may look a whole lot lower than they really are. Look at the whole compensation package before you conclude that one firm is less expensive than another. And be certain the fee schedule is consistent with the regulatory requirements in your state and with postal regulations.

If these considerations don't do the trick, there's one more that may decide the question once and for all:

Which of the consultants you're considering is most likely to understand your strategy, and to help you reach *your* goals (not just their own)?

If you find the right firm, you may be squarely on track toward your strategic goals. Now all you have to do is figure out how to work with the consultant you've selected.

Making the relationship work

Managing a consultant

As a client of a direct mail fundraising firm, you can exert considerable control in four ways:

1. Creative responsibility— You have to expect (and you should insist on) being involved in the fundamental creative decisions. It's your responsibility as much as the consultant's to develop a marketing plan that meets your organization's strategic needs, and to devise marketing concepts for individual mailings that fairly reflect the overall strategy. No matter how much you may rely on your consultant for solid advice on both creative and technical matters, you (or a key staff member) must maintain an overview of the program on a continuing basis.

2. Management style— If you've hired a firm to manage your direct mail program, let them do the job. Ask questions and insist on signing off on all major decisions—but don't micro-manage their work, as though you don't need their help except as messengers between you and the printer. You've got better things to do than to second-guess their segmentations or argue constantly about type sizes or ink colors. If over an extended period they haven't produced acceptable results—or you just don't like the way they represent you to the world—fire them and find another firm.

3. Planning and scheduling— If direct mail is going to work for you, you'll have to mail again and again on a consistent schedule. This means you'll have to resist the perfectionist temptation to rewrite or redesign every appeal or to insist on waiting an extra few weeks before the last trickle of test results confirm a decision to roll out a new package. Occasionally, caution and extra attention to detail are important enough to delay a mailing—*but not very often.* One of the most important things your direct mail consultant can do for you is to help you work out a long-term mailing schedule—and stick to it. If they're missing maildates right and left (and it's not your fault), it's time to reexamine the relationship.

4. Trust— Your consultant is not the enemy. While it's important that financial aspects of the relationship be conducted at arm's length and with all due consideration for what is legal and proper, it's counterproductive to nitpick every bill and question every minor departure from the mailing budget. If the company is taking advantage of you, or consistently overspending by significant amounts, by all means take them to task. It's probably time to look for an alternative. As a structive alternative. It's demoralizing for a consultant to face the third degree about every minor decision—and ultimately you'll pay the price.

The relationship between you and your direct mail consultant is a two-way proposition, and you're responsible for making the most of it—because you're footing the bill. But, in many ways, the burden will be on the company you hire. Your consultants won't just be managing the work they've contracted to do for you. They'll also have to manage their relationship with you.

Managing a client

In some consulting firms, account management responsibilities are widely shared. An "account executive" may be charged with coordinating all of a client's work but turns to others when decisions need to be made. By contrast, at Mal Warwick & Associates and many other firms, "client consultants" are accountable for the success or failure of a client's mailing program. Their job description follows:

1. Strategic planning and analysis

■ Be familiar with the terms of the client's contract and with the provisions of any proposal or marketing plan.

■ Review the long-term direct mail schedule once a month, updating it at least quarterly, and obtain the client's approval for each update.

■ Analyze the results of each mailing, especially testing data, so you're sure they're reflected in the design of future mailings.

■ Take the fullest possible advantage of your client's donor lists with frequent and varied donor renewal and special appeal programs specially tailored to the client's program.

■ Prepare timely statistical reports for the client, and help interpret the data.

2. Copywriting and package design

■ Initiate creative meetings or seek counsel to help determine the marketing strategy.

■ Develop a marketing concept for each mailing and work with the copywriter and designer to ensure that the concept is properly executed and that the resulting package adequately reflects the client's program as well as budgetary limitations.

■ Take full advantage of potential marketing opportunities through aggressive package and price testing.

3. Management and coordination

■ Stay in close contact with the client, and discuss plans and program performance as often as needed, but at least monthly.

■ Obtain timely client approvals for budget, copy, art, and donor file segmentations.

■ Be aware at all times of the status of production work and list acquisition on every project in order to certify that schedules are being met (or to notify the client in advance if they're not).

■ Seek to ensure that the client's mailing list is properly maintained and managed, that caging, cashiering, and donor acknowledgment services are adequately performed, and that useful and accurate reports to track each mailing are generated and delivered.

■ Maintain close communication with any telephone fundraising firm, computer service bureau, or other major program vendor.

4. Financial oversight

■ Draft, monitor, and update the budget for each mailing.

■ Monitor each client's payments to head off financial problems before they develop.

5. Overall marketing and management

■ Take advantage of new opportunities for the client—whether they result from events reported on the evening news, changing circumstances in clients' organizations, or trends in the returns from direct mail campaigns.

■ Pay close attention to clients' mailing programs. Identify and avoid major errors or problems, even if that means stopping work on a mailing that might lose the client money, delaying a maildate to head off significant design or production problems, or testing a new package because the old one isn't meeting the program's goals.

If you're lucky enough to find a consultant who'll do all this for you—and you cooperate fully—you'll be well on the way to getting the most from your direct mail fundraising program.

With skill, patience, adequate investment, and a little luck, you'll be able to derive full value from your organization's resources and multiply your impact.

By making the right strategic choices—and using state-of-the-art direct mail techniques to further your strategic goals—you'll become part of a revolution that has already worked profound changes on American society.

Glossary

ACCOUNT EXECUTIVE. The individual who manages a client's direct mail fundraising activities on behalf of a consulting firm. (Also known as CLIENT CONSULTANT.)

ACQUISITION MAILING. A mailing to prospects to "acquire" new donors, members, or subscribers (also called PROSPECT MAILING).

ACTIVE DONOR. A DONOR whose last gift to an organization was received within the past twelve months (in some organizations, within thirteen, eighteen, or twenty-four months).

ANNUAL APPEAL. For organizations with inactive direct mail fundraising programs, the year's single or principal fundraising appeal, typically mailed at the end or the beginning of the calendar year.

ASK, or ASK AMOUNT. Generally, the minimum (or most heavily emphasized) individual gift suggested in a fundraising PACKAGE. Not the total amount asked of all DONORS.

ATTRITION. The loss of donors due to death, illness, address changes, changing fortunes, or changing priorities.

BACK-END PREMIUM. A free gift offered in exchange for a donation (generally, a donation above a certain minimum amount).

BACK-END SERVICES. The part of the direct mail campaign concerned with CAGING, CASHIERING, tabulating the results, sending DONOR ACKNOWLEDGMENTS, or fulfilling promises made in the mailing, as well as with storing and updating the list of respondents.

BUCKSLIP. A small slip of paper (3-1/2 x 8-1/2 inches is a common size) that fits into the PACKAGE and illustrates some particular feature of the OFFER, such as a free calendar or book promised in return for gifts above a certain minimum amount.

BULK MAIL. Third class mail, which requires a minimum of 200 identical pieces per mailing. Qualifying nonprofit organizations pay discounted rates, currently about three-quarters those paid by business mailers.

BUSINESS REPLY ENVELOPE (BRE). A self-addressed envelope that guarantees payment of postage on receipt by the organization that prints it. (Also called POSTAGE-PAID ENVELOPE).

CAGING. Recording and tallying the raw information from direct mail, telephone fundraising, or other DIRECT RESPONSE campaigns so that the responses may be analyzed and decisions made about future campaigns. Information tallied includes the identity of each donor, the date and amount of each gift and its source. Called "caging" after 19th Century "post office desks," with their multiple cubbyholes or "cages" into which mail was sorted and classified.

CARRIER ENVELOPE. The outside envelope that contains the appeal letter and other components of the direct mail PACKAGE. Also known as an "outer" or "carrier."

CASHIERING. Processing and depositing contributions mailed in response to a direct mail, TELEPHONE FUNDRAISING, or other DIRECT RESPONSE campaign.

CHESHIRE LABEL. A strip of plain paper on which the addressee's name and address are imprinted by computer. Usually printed four across a sheet. Derived from the brand name of a widely-used machine that addresses, cuts, and glues the labels onto envelopes or RESPONSE DEVICES. Still one of the most common forms of addressing in direct mail fundraising (although fast being supplanted by ink-jet or LASER-PRINTING techniques).

CLIENT CONSULTANT. (Also known as ACCOUNT EXECUTIVE.) An employee of a consulting agency who manages a client's direct mail fundraising activities on the firm's behalf.

CLOSED-FACE ENVELOPE. An envelope that does not have a window. (See also WINDOW ENVELOPE.)

COMPILED LIST. A mailing list derived from publicly accessible sources such as directories, telephone books, or city and county records. Contrast with DONOR LIST.

CONTINUATION MAILING. A mailing to larger quantities of prospective donors on lists that have been tested first in modest quantities. (See also ROLL-OUT).

CONTROL PACKAGE. A direct mail acquisition PACKAGE that has performed successfully and against which any new ACQUISITION package is tested.

COPY PLATFORM. A concept on the basis of which a direct mail PACKAGE is to be written. Usually spells out the ASK, the OFFER, the opening lines of the appeal letter, and the envelope TEASER language, if any.

COPYWRITING. The creative process involved in conceiving, designing, and writing a fundraising PACKAGE. Alternatively, the actual wording of the fundraising appeal.

CORE DONORS or MAXI-DONORS. Those DONORS who have recently and/or frequently given generous contributions.

DATABASE. A LIST of names, addresses and other information (in fundraising, especially the giving history) maintained on a computer in such a way that selections may be made or the list ordered on the basis of numerous criteria. Sometimes, a database combines several lists on the basis of some common factor, such as source, into one merged, master list from which duplicates are eliminated.

DEMOGRAPHICS. The study of statistical data about groups of people, especially such characteristics as age, income, gender, religious affiliation, and educational level.

DIRECT RESPONSE. A form of advertising that elicits a direct action by the recipient of the message. The advertising may be a letter, telephone call, newspaper or magazine ad, or a radio or television spot. Normally asks for response by mail or telephone.

DONOR. An individual who has contributed money to a nonprofit organization. Gifts are not necessarily tax-deductible by the donor.

DONOR ACKNOWLEDGMENT. Acknowledges a DONOR'S contribution with a receipt and/or a thank-you letter or note, possibly with other inserts.

DONOR ACQUISITION COST. The difference between the cost of the mailing and the amount it generated in contributions, divided by the number of DONORS acquired. Usually expressed in dollars and cents per donor acquired.

DONOR BASE. The list of an organization's contributors.

DONOR CONVERSION. The process of persuading DONORS who have responded to an organization's PROSPECT MAILINGS with an initial gift to become active, regular, or frequent donors to the organization.

DONOR CULTIVATION. A long-term process through which a nonprofit organization acquaints selected DONORS with its work and becomes better acquainted with the donors' needs and preferences, in hopes of eventually securing large donations.

DONOR FILE. Also donor list. A computer listing, or DATABASE, of the names, addresses, sources, and contribution history of an organization's donors. Sometimes contains additional information, if available.

DONOR RECOGNITION. Any means by which a nonprofit organization publicly acknowledges a DONOR'S support. Examples are plaques and certificates, listings in newsletters or annual reports, screen credit in films and video presentations, and mention at public events.

DONOR RESEARCH. Generally refers to the process of searching through information available to the general public (from such sources as newspapers, magazines, and directories) to unearth facts about an organization's best specific, individual prospective DONORS of MAJOR GIFTS. Contrast with MARKET RESEARCH, which aims at groups of donors rather than individuals.

DONOR RESOLICITATION. An organization's letter or phone call requesting additional support from individuals who have previously supported its work. (Also called SPECIAL APPEAL or, sometimes, RENEWAL).

DONOR RETENTION. The ability to maintain individuals as active and continuing DONORS to an organization. Also, the process of seeking that end.

DONOR SURVEY. An in-depth, quantitative study of the beliefs, attitudes, DEMOGRAPHIC, and PSYCHOGRAPHIC characteristics of an organization's DONORS by means of statistically valid survey research techniques applied to a small sample of the DONOR BASE.

DUPE RATE. The percentage of names identified as duplicates or invalid addresses; also known as the MERGE FACTOR.

80-20 RULE. The maxim that the top twenty percent of an organization's DONORS contribute approximately eighty percent of its revenue, while the bottom eighty percent of the donors contribute just twenty percent. Also called the Pareto Principle.

ELECTRONIC FUNDS TRANSFER (EFT). A method whereby individual DONORS may instruct their banks to make automatic monthly or quarterly deductions from their accounts, which are transferred electronically to the accounts of the charitable organizations of their choice.

ELECTRONIC MAIL. A computerized system that prints, personalizes, and distributes written fundraising appeals with great speed. Usually used for urgent appeals.

FIBER OPTICS. A telecommunications medium that transmits digital information in the form of pulses of laser light through minute strands of transparent cable. Now coming into wide use across the United States, fiber optics is expected to be universally used to transmit both voice and data over long distances in the 21st Century.

FILE. A computerized LIST.

FLASHCOUNT. A periodic statistical report of the results of an individual mailing that summarizes the returns for each list or KEYCODE by percent response, average contribution, and other measures during a particular period of time, usually no more than a few months.

FOCUS GROUP. A method of qualitative research in which a small group (usually eight to twelve) of DONORS or PROSPECTS are methodically interviewed and led through group discussion about their attitudes and reactions toward an organization or the materials it produces.

FORMAT. The size, shape, and color of the envelope, the character of the inserts, and the extent (or lack) of PERSONALIZATION of a direct mail PACKAGE.

FORMER DONORS. Donors who have not contributed to an organization in two or more years (three years or more, for some organizations).

FREQUENCY. The number of times an individual has contributed to an organization, either cumulatively or within a specific period of time.

FRONT-END PREMIUM. An item included in a direct mail PACKAGE as an up-front "free" gift in order to encourage response. Typical front-end premiums are membership cards, stickers, decals, stamps, keychains, address labels, and letter-openers.

FULFILLMENT RATE. The percentage of DONORS who actually send in checks in response to a TELEPHONE FUNDRAISING campaign or other fundraising effort which elicits PLEDGES rather than immediate cash gifts.

FUNDRAISING RATIO. The ratio of cost to revenue, expressed as a percentage. Also, the cost of a dollar raised expressed in dollars and cents. A traditional method used to evaluate the efficiency of fundraising programs.

GEODEMOGRAPHICS. In fundraising, a method of targeting PROSPECTIVE DONORS based on the demographic characteristics revealed in U.S. Census data for residents of specific geographic areas, selected on the basis that their demographic profile closely matches that of an organization's previous DONORS. See also PSYCHOGRAPHICS.

GIFT CLUB or GIVING CLUB. An association or category established by a nonprofit organization that is limited to DONORS who contribute frequent or generous gifts, often receiving special benefits and/or DONOR REC-OGNITION.

GIFT LEVEL. Generally, a measure of an individual DONOR'S capacity for future gifts based on the size of her past contributions. Such measurements may include the amount of the highest previous contribution, the total cumulative amount of all gifts received to date, or the amount of the most recent contribution.

HIGH-DOLLAR MAILING. Direct mail fundraising PACKAGES specifically designed to elicit above-average gifts, by using larger envelopes, extensive personalization, and a high ASK, and mailed to very selective lists.

HOUSE FILE or HOUSE LIST. Names and addresses of an organization's active and recently lapsed DONORS, members, supporters, and subscribers.

IMPACT PRINTER. A computer-driven printing mechanism in which metal or plastic characters directly strike the paper. Impact printers include "daisy-wheel" machines that make a typewriter-like impression, and "line printers" that operate at very high speed and leave an often sketchy impression on the page, commonly associated with computer printers.

INDEPENDENT SECTOR. The term denoting the nonprofit world—that is, organizations that are neither governmental nor profit-making businesses. (A coalition of nonprofit organizations also operates under this name.) Also THIRD SECTOR.

INK-JET PRINTING. Printing (generally of a name, address, and KEYCODE) executed by a high-speed printer that produces an image by spraying ink through small jets to imitate typewriter print.

INQUIRIES. In fundraising, individuals who have responded to an advertisement or a direct mail package with a request for information or a response to a survey but have not sent contributions.

INVOLVEMENT DEVICE. An element in a direct mail PACKAGE used to heighten interest in the package and to provide recipients with opportunities to use their hands or to participate in some way to assist the mailer. Common examples are petitions, "surveys," post cards addressed to decision-makers, stamps, and stickers.

KEYCODE. A code consisting of letters and/or numbers assigned to a specific LIST or segment of a list to track responses. Its purpose is to evaluate the list's effectiveness relative to other lists. Usually printed on the mailing label or RESPONSE DEVICE. See also SOURCE CODE.

LAPSED DONORS. DONORS whose last gift arrived at least a year to eighteen months ago but no longer than two to three years ago. In some organizations, they're called LYBUNTS ("Last Year But Unfortunately Not This Year").

LASER PRINTING. In direct mail fundraising, a PERSONALIZED process of reproducing printed material that combines photocopier technology with computerized LIST MAINTENANCE techniques, permitting each sheet or printed impression to include information unique to one individual on a DONOR FILE.

LETTERSHOP. Sometimes called a "mailhouse." The shop in which the individual components of a mailing are collated, inserted, and packaged for delivery to the post office. Lettershops also frequently address and affix postage to the mailing PACKAGES.

LIFETIME VALUE or LONG-TERM VALUE. Refers to the long-term value of a DONOR, member, subscriber, or buyer from an organization's perspective. Calculated by one of several methods, this value provides guidance when setting investment levels in ACQUISITION MAIL.

LIFT LETTER. A second or supplementary letter included in a fundraising PACKAGE to reinforce the message of the main letter or present an argument for a contribution from a different point of view. Often signed by a celebrity or other influential individual.

LIST. In direct mail, a DATABASE of names and addresses of individuals who share one or more characteristics, such as membership in a given organization.

LIST BROKER. An agent who manages the relationship between LIST OWNERS and mailers, arranging the rental or exchange of mailing LISTS (in whole or part). Although the principal parties are the actual list owner and list user, the list broker acts on behalf of the mailer to make all necessary arrangements with the LIST MANAGER, who acts as the agent for the list user.

LIST EXCHANGE. An exchange of donor, member, or subscriber LISTS between two organizations, generally on a name-for-name basis, with the two organizations usually mailing at different times.

LIST MAINTENANCE. The ongoing process of updating and correcting a DONOR FILE or other computerized mailing LIST.

LIST MANAGER. The organization or individual, often a LIST BROKER or direct mail consultant, who is responsible for the promotion and record-keeping necessary for the regular exchange or rental of a mailing list.

LIST OWNER. The organization or individual that owns rental or exchange rights to a mailing LIST.

LIST RENTAL. The arrangement through which a LIST OWNER furnishes names for one-time use only to a mailer.

LIST TEST. A random sampling of a LIST used to determine the cost-effectiveness of mailing to the entire list. In most fundraising applications, list tests are based on samples of between 3,000 and 10,000 names.

LIVE STAMP. An actual postage stamp affixed by hand or machine, usually either to a CARRIER ENVELOPE or to a reply envelope.

MAGNETIC TAPE. An early but now universally accepted electronic storage medium favored in the direct mail industry to record and reproduce via computer the data on a mailing LIST.

MAIL-RESPONSIVENESS. The propensity for an individual to respond to a sales offer or funding appeal sent by mail.

MAJOR GIFT. A significant and out-of-the-ordinary gift, which may be as little as $100 for some organizations or upwards of $1,000,000 for others.

MARKET. The intended audience of an appeal. The likely or potential supporters of an organization. The prospect LISTS that together comprise an organization's UNIVERSE.

MARKET RESEARCH. In fundraising, refers to DONOR SURVEYS, FOCUS GROUPS, and other methods used to study the beliefs, attitudes, DEMOGRAPHIC, and PSYCHOGRAPHIC characteristics of previous or potential donors, in order to understand how to devise and deliver more effective appeals for support.

MARKETING CONCEPT. The concept on which a fundraising PACKAGE is based. A capsule statement of the connection between the OFFER, the MARKET, and the signer of the appeal letter.

MAXI-DONORS or CORE DONORS. Those DONORS who have recently and/or frequently given generous contributions.

MEMBERSHIP RENEWAL. A RESOLICITATION, used by organizations with formal membership structures, requesting payment of an individual's annual dues. Alternatively, a response to a dues notice, or a system to collect dues from the membership as a whole.

MERGE/PURGE. A computer operation that combines two or more mailing LISTS in a matching process to produce one FILE that is relatively free of duplicates. Also measures and produces a report on the degree to which the component lists overlap with each other.

MERGE DUPES. Also MULTI-DONORS. DONORS, members or subscribers found on more than one PROSPECT LIST. In commercial direct mail, called MULTI-BUYERS.

MERGE FACTOR. The percentage of names identified as duplicates or bad addresses; also known as the DUPE RATE.

MULTI-BUYERS. See MULTI-DONORS.

MULTI-DONORS. Also MERGE DUPES. DONORS, members or subscribers found on more than one PROSPECT LIST. In commercial direct mail, called MULTI-BUYERS.

NET PRESENT VALUE. In assessing the worth in current dollars of anticipated future revenue, the projected value is discounted to take into effect the rate of inflation, or prevailing rates of return on investment, or some combination of those two factors.

NONPROFIT SECTOR. See INDEPENDENT SECTOR or THIRD SECTOR.

OFFER. In fundraising, the programmatic action and/or individual benefits promised by an organization to those who send contributions, dues, or subscription payments. Also known as the "pitch." Commercially, the terms under which a specific product or service is promoted by a mailer. In fundraising, the offer is the set of needs, promises, or assurances that justifies the ASK.

ON-LINE PACKAGING. A production method that integrates printing, PERSONALIZATION, and bundling for the post office into one continuous process on an assembly line.

PACKAGE. A direct mail appeal, its wrapping, and all its contents. Commonly consists of a CARRIER ENVELOPE, a letter, a RESPONSE DEVICE, and a BUSINESS REPLY ENVE-LOPE (BRE). May include other items, such as a brochure, news clipping, or a FRONT-END PREMIUM.

PACKAGE TEST. Testing one direct mail PACKAGE (or one of its features or characteristics) against those of another by mailing both to statistically equivalent groups of individuals chosen at random from the same LIST or lists.

PERSONALIZATION. The reproduction of a message on individualized materials that bear the recipient's name and (often) other unique, personal information as well. Methods include LASER PRINTING, INK-JET PRINTING, and other computer-driven technologies.

PILOT MAILING. See TEST MAILING.

PLANNED GIVING. Using estate planning methods to formulate and schedule contributions by an individual DONOR, generally involving large or long-term gifts or bequests.

PLEDGE. In fundraising, a promise made by a DONOR or PROSPECT to contribute money at a later time. Both the amount and the date when the gift will be made may be either specified or unspecified. Used as either noun or verb.

PLEDGE CARD. Also called pledge reminder. In TELEPHONE FUNDRAISING, a notice sent to remind those who PLEDGE to contribute to an organization. A REPLY ENVE-LOPE is almost always enclosed.

PLEDGE PROGRAM. A system, often a GIFT CLUB, through which ardent supporters of a nonprofit organization may give regular, generally monthly, donations and often receive special benefits in return. Can be implemented manually or through ELECTRONIC FUNDS TRANSFER. (Sometimes called SUSTAINER PROGRAM.)

POSTAGE-PAID ENVELOPE. A self-addressed envelope that guarantees payment of postage on receipt by the organization that prints it. Also called BUSINESS REPLY ENVELOPE (BRE).

PREDICTIVE DIALING. A computer-driven system widely used in telemarketing to automate the dialing of telephone numbers. Increases the number of caller contacts per hour.

PREMIUM. A product offered or given to a prospective DONOR, member, or subscriber as an incentive to respond to a direct mail PACK-AGE. See BACK-END PREMIUM and FRONT-END PREMIUM.

PRESSURE-SENSITIVE LABELS.
Mailing labels, generally affixed by hand, that do not require water. Colloquially called "peel-off" or "peel-and-stick" labels.

PROSPECT. In direct mail fundraising, a prospective new DONOR. In MAJOR GIFT fundraising, any prospective donor, including an organization's previous contributors. See also QUALIFIED PROSPECT.

PROSPECT MAILING. A mailing to prospective new DONORS, members, or subscribers to ask for their support; also called ACQUISITION MAILING or "cold mail."

PSYCHOGRAPHICS. In fundraising, a method of targeting prospective DONORS based on their demonstrated (or predicted) lifestyle choices or behavioral traits. See also GEODEMOGRAPHICS.

QUALIFIED PROSPECT. A prospective DONOR whose interest has been established through a letter of inquiry, response to an advertisement, a telephoned request for information, or attendance at an event.

RECENCY. The date (or time period) during which a DONOR'S latest contribution was received.

RESOLICITATION or RENEWAL MAILING.
An organization's letter or phone call requesting additional support from individuals who have previously supported its work. Also called SPECIAL APPEAL or DONOR RESOLICITATION.

RESPONSE or REPLY DEVICE. A form, generally restating the OFFER and bearing the addressee's name and address and a KEYCODE, on which the recipient is asked to indicate the size of her gift and sometimes other information as well.

ROLL-OUT. Generally, a mailing to larger quantities of prospective DONORS on LISTS that have been tested first in modest quantities. More precisely, using all available names remaining on one or more pretested lists in a CONTINUATION MAILING.

SEEDING (or SALTING) LISTS. A practice employed by LIST OWNERS and LIST BROKERS for protection against misuse or theft. Names and addresses, usually fictitious, are inserted on the LIST so that the owner or broker receives copies of all mailings sent to the list.

SEGMENTATION. The process of subdividing a LIST into subdivisions or "segments." Most commonly defined by RECENCY, FREQUENCY, GIFT LEVEL, or SOURCE (or some combination of these variables).

SELF-MAILER. A direct mail PACKAGE that requires no separate CARRIER ENVELOPE. Usually either a piece of paper with multiple folds or a booklet format.

SERVICE BUREAU. A company that offers BACK-END SERVICES, typically including a variety of data processing services.

SOURCE. The LIST on which a DONOR's name and other data were originally obtained.

SOURCE CODE. A KEYCODE denoting the specific LIST or segment of a list from which a DONOR's name and address were originally derived.

SPECIAL APPEAL. An appeal for funds from previous DONORS or members that is not a MEMBERSHIP RENEWAL notice. Many organizations send special appeals several times per year.

SPLIT TEST. A test of any variable in a mailing (such as PACKAGE variations, the ASK, or different postage rates). One or more LISTS or segments are split into equal numbers of statistically identical names and addresses to determine which approach works better than others. Also called an "A/B split."

SUSTAINER PROGRAM. A GIFT CLUB through which ardent supporters of a nonprofit organization may give regular, generally monthly, donations and often receive special benefits and/or DONOR RECOGNITION. Can be implemented either manually or through ELECTRONIC FUNDS TRANSFER. Also known as PLEDGE PROGRAM.

TEASER. A brief message on the CARRIER ENVELOPE used to pique the reader's interest or curiosity and thus increase the likelihood that the envelope will be opened.

TELEPHONE FUNDRAISING. Calling previous DONORS or prospective donors by phone to ask for donations. The application of telemarketing techniques to the NONPROFIT SECTOR.

TESTING. The process of comparing results for dissimilar items by simultaneously mailing each item to an equal number of statistically identical names. For statistical validity, changes in only one variable may be assessed in any one test. The impact of different rates of postage, suggested minimum gift amounts, TEASERS, or other variables may be compared in this manner.

TEST MAILING. An organization's initial effort to gauge its potential to mount a cost-effective direct mail fundraising program. Sometimes called a PILOT MAILING.

THIRD SECTOR. Term denoting the nonprofit world—that is, organizations that are neither governmental agencies nor profit-making businesses. Also called the INDEPENDENT SECTOR or NONPROFIT SECTOR.

UNIQUE NAMES. Those names and addresses remaining on a merged or combined mailing LIST for a PROSPECT MAILING after a MERGE/PURGE has identified and eliminated duplicates and invalid addresses.

UNIVERSE. The total number of names and addresses that comprise a mailing LIST. Also, the total number of names and addresses judged to be good prospects to support a nonprofit organization or political committee.

UPDATING. Adding, changing, or deleting information on a DONOR LIST to increase its accuracy.

UPGRADING. The process of inducing previous DONORS to increase the amount or FREQUENCY of their gifts.

WINDOW ENVELOPE. An envelope that reveals the name and address through a die-cut hole, or window. An envelope may have more than one window to show other features of the enclosed material.

WORD-PROCESSING. In direct mail, generally refers to PERSONALIZATION that employs IMPACT PRINTERS to mimic individually typed letters.

About the author

MAL WARWICK heads four affiliated companies that provide a wide range of fundraising and marketing services to clients throughout America. Widely recognized as a national leader in direct mail and telephone fundraising, he is the author of five books, writes a monthly column and edits a newsletter, and is a popular public speaker and workshop leader.

Writing

This book, originally titled *Revolution in the Mailbox: How Direct Mail Fundraising Is Changing the Face of American Society—And How Your Organization Can Benefit*, was first published by Strathmoor Press in 1990. The first of Mal's five books, it has been recognized as a standard in the field.

Mal's latest book, *How to Write Successful Fundraising Letters* (1994), has received rave notices from *Library Journal, Booklist, The Baltimore Sun*, and other mainstream reviewers as well as numerous nonprofit trade publications.

Mal also writes a monthly column on direct mail fundraising ("The Warwick File") for *The NonProfit Times*. He edits (and Strathmoor Press publishes) a bimonthly subscription newsletter, *Successful Direct Mail & Telephone Fundraising*.

Consulting services

Mal is chairman of Mal Warwick & Associates, Inc. (Berkeley, California), which he established in 1979. The firm specializes in direct mail fundraising for nonprofit organizations. He is also co-founder and chairman of The Progressive Group, Inc. (Hadley, Massachusetts), which offers telephone fundraising services, and founder and president of Response Management Technologies, Inc. (Berkeley, California), a provider of back-end services.

Clients of Mal's affiliated companies have included the American Red Cross, Bread for the World, the Environmental Defense Fund, Baylor University Medical Foundation, and more than 300 other nationwide and regional public interest organizations and charities, as well as five major Democratic Presidential candidates.

Through Changing America, Inc., Mal operates EditEXPRESS™ and Strathmoor Press and undertakes occasional consulting assignments. His personal clients have included the Environmental Defense Fund, Apple Computer, Inc., the Salvation Army, the University of California at Davis, the Jewish Community Federation of San Francisco, Rodale Press, and Camp Fire Boys & Girls.

Mal is Chairman of the Association of Direct Response Fundraising Counsel, the national association of direct mail fundraising consultants, and is a member of the National Society of Fund Raising Executives (NSFRE).

Since 1969, Mal has been a resident of Berkeley, California. He co-founded the Berkeley Community Fund of the San Francisco Foundation in 1992 and is currently its chair. He was a 1963 graduate of the University of Michigan, attended Columbia University for two years, and served as a Peace Corps Volunteer in Ecuador from 1965 to 1969.

Index